Songs In The Spirit :
A Collection

by
Marlena Tanya Muchnick

For further information, contact the author at:
www.jewishconvert-lds.com; or, www.peopleofthebook-judaica.com

Book design and cover photo-illustration by Kim Cooney dba Byzintek
15843 SE 47th Street, Bellevue, Washington 98006-3264 USA
kim.cooney@comcast.net; www.byzintek.com; 425.643.2330
Image credits: O'Brien Productions/BrandX/Getty Images, Paul Edmondson/Getty Images

Published by Granite Publishing & Distribution, LLC
868 North 1430 West, Orem Utah 84057 USA
Toll-free 1.800.574.5779, Tel. 801.229.9023, Fax 801.229.1924

Printed in the United States of America

꽃

Marlena Tanya Muchnick is a Jewish convert to the Church and was baptized a Latter-day Saint April 6, 1988. She lives in Western Washington state.

Marlena gives firesides throughout America about her conversion experience, her testimony and her fervent love for the Savior. These talks convey helpful information about Judaism. She also enjoys presenting Seminary and Institute talks as well as informal informational gatherings and Passover Seder demonstrations. Please visit her web site to set up a presentation in your ward, stake, or mission.

Marlena's published soft cover books, tapes, CD's and songs are available through LDS and other bookstores online, and from the author through her web sites (see at left). These currently include:

꽃 Notes of A Jewish Convert to the LDS Church: Conversion of A Soul

꽃 Life Changing Testimonies of the Lord Jesus Christ

꽃 Adventures With the Angels of Love

꽃 People of The Book (Am ha-Sefer Torah). Also available in tape and CD set

꽃 A Mormon's Guide to Judaism

꽃 Mashiach of Brodskii Street: Terror in Berdichev, 1941
     (Written under the surname Simkovitz)

꽃 Dynamics of Freedom: 7-½ hour sessions on Constitution. VHS

꽃 Fireside addresses with original songs: DVD and tape for libraries and
     showings to congregations

꽃 Original songs with sheet music

꽃 Demo (on DVD) for preview by those interested in scheduling visits.
     Excerpts from fireside talks, songs, Passover seder demonstration and
     the nature of Judaism.

Preface: On the 15th Anniversary of My Baptism —

Today, April 6, 2003, is the fifteenth anniversary of my baptism into The Church of Jesus Christ of Latter-day Saints. It has been a day and night of deep reflection. I am a Jew, with a heritage in the Ukraine, where my father was born and where my mother's folks were born. My earliest memories are of the synagogue and the teachings I received therein. The very idea of Christianity was forbidden in my home, and I was always discouraged from having much to do with those not of my faith. Fortunately, I learned some basics of the full Gospel in my studies of Judaism.

I grew up in an abusive home. I ran away from that environment many times before I was able to support myself. I encountered and wrestled with many overwhelming problems that lay in store for me. Somehow, during those confusing years I managed to educate myself and obtain good employment, but I also suffered the effects of depression, anxiety, of homelessness and loneliness. I was always plagued with deep insecurities. My writing ability, a gift I discovered early in life, was without purpose of intent or direction, a further frustration. I married and divorced more than once. Religious life became a thing of the past. I suffered through some humiliating times and put myself in the way of dangerous circumstances which threatened my life and deeply scarred my emotional wellbeing. I was not able to successfully direct myself. I knew no peace nor joy nor trust in what the world had shown me. I contemplated ending my life. In short, I needed help which only the Lord could render.

It was through a series of remarkable events that I was led to finally examine my life as I reached maturity. Those events involved numerous souls who contributed their knowledge and help.

My first book, *Notes of A Jewish Convert to the LDS Church: Conversion of a Soul* tells my story. It took a number of years for the disparate parts of my life and work to come together, including the visit of a holy messenger, but in 1988 I stepped into the waters of baptism administered by one having authority, to be born anew. I became a Jew fulfilled, free of my past's baggage, free to make a new and correct estimation of my gifts and to join with the Lord in reassessing my possibilities for growth, success and happiness.

The results are no less than staggering to me. I have truly become a new person within my heart, mind and spirit. I embrace the peace that my Christ brings to me. I have the blessings of the priesthood, an enduring marriage. The temples of God are my constant refuge. I am deeply and forever grateful for the changes that have been wrought in me. I thank my Heavenly Father for saving my life and providing work and direction for me through dedication to his purposes for time and eternity. My love for my Savior and Redeemer fills my spirit with love and joy. I know that I am a child of God. I do not worry, for I am learning that "There is no fear in love; but perfect love casteth out fear..." (1 John 4:18).

There is no secret to success as a person on this earth. In following the teachings of all our prophets with a clean and honest heart, having faith in Heavenly Father and Jesus Christ, human potential will be maximized and eternal joy attained. I am a mere child of 15 now, a teenager in the Gospel, in the fertile fields of the Lord, free to grow, to love, to succeed in my purposes because they are also His purposes. Often the path to perfection seems clouded, but it is there if searched out, sure and perfectly reachable.

On my 15th anniversary, I give thanks for my membership in the Lord's Church. I look forward to endless lifetimes of benefits.

— *Marlena Tanya Muchnick (Baker)*

This book is for

Sharon

who brings the world

her gift of love

First Message —

All that comes from the Father
Goes back to the Father.

We are a product of His love
And we shall return in glory
If we are faithful.

And the meaning of life
And the meaning of death
Is in eternal
rebirth.

In Jesus' name, amen.

Received June 7, 1991; 10:20 am

CONTENTS

ESSAYS

A Pilgrim's Progression —

You must be the change you wish to see in the world. — *Mahatma Gandhi*

There is ever increasing reason for me to believe that each event in our lives is a provident opportunity for growth. The merest reflection on the simple fact that a soul can chart its growth and refinement from childhood even to one's teenaged years is to me silent avowal of the Lord's plan for our progression toward the perfection of our personalities.

Remembering thoughts from childhood barely into the twentieth year of my life, I imagined becoming that irresponsible, carefree adult of my dreams because in those shadowy years every day was a challenge, a painful reminder of some necessary adjustment that makes adulthood almost a relief. It is a wonder that I eventually fostered a narrow and cautious focus to my own life. In search of profound understanding of my Judaic heritage I discovered that path lay in true Christianity, in a church baptism, in proselytizing missionary work, and eventually in book publication!

Truly, I have been accompanied to these stations along my path, as we all are, befriended and encouraged by those unseen though vigilant spirits of God who have adopted us as their mortal charges. They quietly endure our errors, weep with us through our trials and genuinely rejoice at our rudimentary human accomplishments. These protective spirits will, hopefully, greet us face to face as we cross the gulf of time and circumstance that separates us from the world of spirits which is our destiny. I believe that is when the eternal purposes of our mortal journey will become clear to us and we will be given knowledge that we have in good part — and with the help of those who know far more than we — foreordained much of it ourselves.

When I became nineteen I accompanied a friend on a trip to an old gutted metal mine we had heard of near a once busy junction with the colorful name of Chloride, now only a crow hop in the windy desert of southwest Arizona. It had long been abandoned by the miners who seemed to have fled suddenly (just after lunch?) without stopping to pack or arrange for forwarding of belongings. Browsing around those hundred year old windblown shacks, smelling deeply of the acrid creosote bushes that had grown up around the unused cabins and pilings, I wondered at the grimy plates and cups left upon the tables, books and mirrors left behind, daily use clothes still upon hangers in closets without doors . . . in some cabins I found meat remains on dinner plates.

Moving through the mining area, tools were carelessly thrown, rope lay in abundance, coiled and waiting. Worker's hats, boots and coats still hung in readiness on hooks near the long lavatory that housed filthy toilet stalls without doors. The mounds of metal dust which had hardened to become small calico-colored iron oxide hills of white and rust, were everywhere. The footprints of men busily stomping through the camp were preserved in that powder and honed by the wind. I clumsily followed them back and forth throughout the compound, imagining myself in their shoes, making the rounds with other workers, smiling and sharing the day's hard camaraderie.

I had stumbled upon a forsaken community of assiduous people at work. Surely this place had been often visited in its silences by the curious, but it did not look vandalized. It was a ghost camp, an entity, like a monument we visit, a museum we peruse. Those before us likely had wondered, too, as they viewed the artifacts of an industrious existence in this obscure place. It begged the question: What had really happened here that these people left so suddenly, leaving so much of themselves behind?

I could imagine these miners, their women and children with them — given jolting news one day of the gold mine being played out or of the company in grave danger of going broke — turning to look at one another, quick to discern a lost opportunity but opining new ones. Rising as one, they must have methodically chosen and gathered those few necessary possessions and hurried away to another, more prosperous camp where the men could labor for another day's wage while the wives would strike up another hearth, make another supper.

Finding tables set, clothes hastily thrown upon furniture and sheeted beds still mussed from sleep, I mused that those miner families must have moved as the Israelites fled Egypt, vacating an entire mining camp in a few hours. I reckoned they had, perhaps without another good choice, taken a giant step away from a played out past, having suddenly to unearth whatever new experiences God had set before them to discover. Were they resolute in their hearts?

I still wonder about Chloride. It may be gone from the map but it remains in the terrain of my mind in a curious way because it is where I first came hard to terms with the idea that people are meant to progress in mortality through their experiences, though sometimes that involves leaving behind what is familiar in favor of sudden change in circumstance demanding perseverance. Often this comes without our desire or control. I wonder if these are blessings in disguise, but I am sure now they are necessary for the soul's flowering.

Those members of The Church of Jesus Christ of Latter-day Saints (and a great many non-members) have knowledge and testimony of the travails of the Prophet Joseph Smith who went into a grove of trees one day in his youth in the spring of 1820 to pray about the "right" church sect to join. He was given a vision in which he saw God and Jesus Christ who told him that none were correct. Joseph was further told that he would, through the angel Moroni, be led to buried golden plates which told the story of Christ's visit to the Americas, that he would henceforth be taught the true Gospel of Jesus Christ by angelic witnesses, that he would be instrumental in translating those plates and publishing them as the Book of Mormon, that he had been chosen by God to become the first latter day prophet and that he would restore to the earth God's Church as Christ had led it. He received the restored priesthood that provides for the ministering of angels through God's properly appointed servants.

Following all this the Prophet Joseph Smith received revelations from the Savior relative to the re-establishing of that Church (See the Doctrine and Covenants), and seems to have written in a day through wondrous inspiration The Thirteen Articles of Faith which define the essential mission of the Saints. He later translated a discovered papyrus containing previously unknown information from the early prophet Abraham which tells of man's pre-earthly existence and throws great light upon the true purpose of Adam and Eve in the Garden and other truths essential to human salvation.

The restoration of the Church led, of course, to the rebuilding of God's holy temples wherein members can take out their endowments, do proxy work for their dead that all may hear the Gospel message, and give instructions for binding together on earth and in heaven for eternity their families, one to another. A simple prayer from a pure and honest heart opened the windows of Heaven after long drought and from them poured the divine knowledge essential to the salvation of the planet.

What would have happened to the world if Joseph Smith had resisted change? We could argue that he read James 1:5 wherein it advises that a soul can obtain wisdom by asking of God, and Joseph greatly desired to make a change for the better in his life. But after receiving his vision he continued for a time to pursue his "common vocations in life" [1] until he felt compelled to "know of my state and standing" [2] before God. We know through reading his story and the millions of unrestrained testimonies of those whose lives were forever altered by what he did, that Joseph Smith, ready or not, shook off his mundane routines and diligently undertook to follow the Lord at all cost to himself and his family. That he became a martyr in his pursuit of truth is only a by-product of his achievements. A true prophet is known by his fruits. So are we all the growers of the lives we lead and so we are given this life that we may produce its varied harvest.

Had the Prophet Joseph Smith not chosen to follow the Lord and accept the callings he was given, another surely would have been chosen. But that person would have had to overcome some similitude of difficult circumstance to bring to fruit the demands of the Lord regarding the restoration of His Church upon the earth, in any dispensation. Personal growth would be unavoidable in the execution of heavenly duties and the perils they always seem to include. The point here is that when we are faced with significant change in our lives, it is a chance to expand our understanding of our purposes in the world and to test our faith and obedience to that divine Power which moves over us in love and which seeks to enlarge us that we might become worthy of our rightful inheritance, mortally and eternally. Change cannot be avoided, but it can be viewed negatively and that leads to the deterioration of the personality. Positive change, then, is growth which transforms us in ways which lead to our progression, hastening us toward greater opportunity and more profound discoveries.

Life is a constant renewal of the exercise of agency. We, as Saints, have been taught that all things typify of Christ. Using his life, death and resurrection as our examples we can deduce that there are treasures waiting for us which are not known until the spade has turned the dirt and the hidden seeds of new life brought forth. In these seeds are waiting the precious opportunities of life for the diligent searcher to unearth. True treasure lies within our growing faith in God and His teachings, for they all lead to the continued discovering of His kingdom within the sacred privacy of our own soul.

It is in that spirit that this essay is written. It is my solemn hope that this story will inspire even in unfledged readers new awareness of possibilities within themselves such that they will yearn toward the exploration of their undiscovered territory, as spirit seedlings of our Heavenly Father. Just as those miners who, leaving behind a secure and happy camp turned their faces toward a new, a sudden beckoning wind and like some angelic seduction followed it to a farther country with a richer soil, a more arable land. Properly planted and lovingly harvested they will reap infinitely sweeter fruit.

---

[1] *Joseph Smith Testimony, HC Vol 1, Ch 1:27*

[2] *op cit. Ch 1:29*

Toward A Perfect Union —

Those who search for meaning in their lives sometimes discover important clues where they would never expect to be enlightened. I recall the day I found what I believe is one of the main principles that define the essential purpose of all scripture. It came about, of course, through my encounter with a word in the Holy Bible.

In chapter 20 of Exodus, second of the Five Books of Moses, 6th verse, Heavenly Father reveals to that Hebrew prophet His commandments to love Him with all our heart, mind and will, knowing that the righteous will "delight . . . in the law of the Lord: . . . " (Psalms 1:2). The restrictions against making or serving "graven images" contains the caveat that those who do so quickly invite the wrath of the Father unto future generations. To those whose obedience is born of love He promises to be merciful, for ". . . the righteous Lord loveth righteousness" (Psalm 11:7).

There are many false images of happiness in this world. How many have we invited into our lives? Do our lamps of faithfulness burn intensely at the threshold of this prophetic 21st century? Do we really know how to love?

Love. The word is mentioned 395 times in the King James Version of the Holy Bible. I am still counting its appearances in the Book of Mormon and other scriptures. Almost every reference I find contains an admonishment that love is best learned when obedience is given to holy teachings and most fully realized when practiced in service to others. But as we stand upon the doorstep of this third century of recorded history, it is all too clear that there is little love and peace in the world arenas or in our private lives. Only when the Savior was on earth did a temporary and tenuous withholding of violence exist. With his murder, Rome again took up the armaments of conflict and other countries entered into battle. Sadly but assuredly, our Father in Heaven and His Host are constant witness to the sins and sorrows of mankind yesterday and today, even as His prophets have continually instructed and chastened us to repent of our willfulness, to choose to love serving God rather than to serve the interests of the world

President Hinckley reflected in the recent General Conference of the Church that we stand upon "the summit of the ages . . ." (Ensign

November 1999, p. 74) the last and final dispensation toward which all in the past has pointed. This year 2005, a time millions around the globe were sure we would never reach, I have a prayer in my heart that in this century all men and women will learn of Christ and will choose to follow the Almighty One through the agency of Jesus Christ. I pray that they will partake of his atoning sacrifice.

We have to work toward these things. When I was still a girl in Hebrew school I revered the rabbi of my congregation. How ingratiating, how strong-willed and affirming he was to all of us. He occasionally called my father into his small synagogue office to visit with him and to offer prayer and counseling. These appointments with my father and other men of the synagogue were a routine but essential part of the rabbi's spiritual progress, as well. A lively man of 80, Rabbi Zalman had counseled many years in that small synagogue, serving numerous heads of Jewish families in a patriarchal "calling". Normally, they met before services, but when he came to the house my mother would pour him a small glass of Mogen David grape wine in appreciation. Rabbi would ceremoniously bow and then beam at us with joy.

Whenever our rabbi received remuneration and/or gratitude for his ministrations he would remark that his purpose was to carry on in the 18th century Ashkenazic (an eastern European) religious movement called Hasidism in which the rabbi — *rebbe* (rebby, teacher) becomes an ecclesiastical director to his congregation. Rabbi Zalman practiced fellowship with many of the *hasid* (hah sid, congregant) in the synagogue. The Hebrew for this program is *yehidut* (yeh he doo). A revered counselor, one looked upon by the congregation as a man chosen of God, Hasidic rabbis strive to develop exclusive relationships of love and support with their hasidim, as earnest intermediaries. The most important goal for all concerned is to forge a strong spiritual bond that will hopefully transcend ordinariness of worship into full blown intimacy with the God of the Jews. The rabbi's essential purpose is to inculcate into his relationships with each hasid a spiritual intimacy, with God as the central figure in that counsel, the bonding agent between man and his destiny.

The unalterable goal, our rabbi told my father, is to bring everyone involved closer to God. A rabbi is a kind of therapist, he is the synagogue's father figure, beloved by his congregation with an almost holy esteem. The rebbe clearly knows what God wants from this work. It is to bring about in the hasid a critical transformation through love and faith, and in the rabbi a clearer discernment of his own life purposes.

For this task the rabbi prepares himself with years of rigorous training and devotion, and has one or more mentors. The ancient ministry of yehidut continues today in Hasidic communities across the world.

Rabbi Zalman accomplished much good with our little family. I know our Heavenly Father sent that special envoy to bring our family closer to Him, just as He saw each of us off to earth to tend our particular garden of relatives, families and friends. Lest we not have time to remember, there are also neighbors, congregations, societies, our country, even our world to consider beside ourselves, all of whom need and expect to be nurtured.

But how to be at one with a planet when most days of our lives seem to revolve around bringing comfort to ourselves? When in our busy lives will we corner a precious fragment of personal time or the energy of spirit and singleness of purpose required of us as ministers of the love that brings peace?

While the Savior was on his earthly ministry many were drawn deeply to him. John the Baptist's love and faith were of such depth that he preached fervently of Jesus' mission as the Savior of mankind, though he had no direct knowledge of how or when that epiphany was to manifest. Martyrdom for that prophet was a gift he lovingly offered as proof of his unwavering testimony. I am always moved by stories of love, especially spiritual love, because in the examples of men of vision such as John the Baptist, Isaiah, Malachi, Ezekiel, those many heroes of the Book of Mormon and the seers and revelators that have led the Restoration, I sense in my own bones their passionate commitment and love for their work. I love most of all the example of our Savior whose path led past the cross to resurrection and life. He walked in innocence and in peace, he taught us love and prepared for us through his unconditional surrender, the way for each of us to overcome the world.

In the third chapter of Ether (Book of Mormon) there is an outstanding example of the power of love. Captain Moroni tells of the marvelous experience of the brother of Jared who was chastised by the Savior for his lack of prayer and supplication. The brother of Jared immediately repents and is then commanded to build barges that he might sail into unknown territory to claim for his inheritance a land "choice above all other lands," a metaphor for eternal life and exaltation. When the brother of Jared complies with the Lord's instructions he cries out,

"And I know, O Lord, that thou hast all power, and can do whatsoever thou wilt for the benefit of man . . ." He gathered stones and asked that Jesus touch them "that they might shine forth in darkness." The Lord complies and the brother of Jared sees clearly the Lord touch each of the stones, bringing them light. He falls down in fear, innocent of knowledge that Jesus has a body, but he is raised and testifies that Christ always speaks truth, whereupon the Savior declares "Because thou knowest these things ye are redeemed from the fall; therefore ye are brought back into my presence; therefore I show myself to you... for never has man believed in me as thou hast. The brother of Jared is shown "the body of the spirit" of Christ. (Ether 3:4-21). When love for God and Christ is complete in man, he finds even greater love and commitment poured out upon him from Deity.

Probably few of us have achieved that degree and intensity of mystical union with our Father in Heaven through the agency of Christ, but it is not an achievement reserved only for prophets, apostles and martyrs of centuries past. True, when they stood for a historic moment at the meeting place of life with death they chose to die rather than renounce their faith or allow it to be diminished. I know that in these coming thousand years we and our posterity are facing far more wondrous and challenging, even cataclysmic times than did those heroes! The coming of the Savior to adjudicate the earth, the restoration to him by Adam of millennial keys, changes in the earth and skies, return of the lost tribes of Israel, a new temple in Jerusalem, millions of Saints doing work in the temples on a 24 hour schedule. And, oh yes, a thousand years of peace.

Father in Heaven has shared His Plan with prophets and revelators who have throughout history warned us unceasingly to fill our lamps with faith, love and charity that we will know the Son of God and will welcome him when he returns in glory. But few of us search the horizon for the coming of the Lord. We live lives of routine and our preoccupations with details and habits dull us for spiritual things, leading us away from study, contemplation of heavenly things and the charity we owe others. Love's intense dynamic and eternal achievement we allow to detour. Desires of the heart become rooted in what is temporal. In the tumbling turmoil of our limited mortality, often weighted down by earthly sorrows, people lose the light of Christ and wander into spiritual darkness. They hearken to the world's many "graven images" in place of the true God and in doing so become lost to the promise that Jesus makes available to every soul.

The Savior knows our pain. Recall the time he fed the five thousand who came to hear him preach near the Sea of Galilee. "I am the bread of life," he said. "He that cometh to me shall never hunger; and he that believeth on me shall never thirst" (John 6:35). Was he only repeating Mosiac Law with a new twist to impress the Jews? Did he come to earth as a man from the presence of God just to give us his message of peace through new philosophy? Did he teach the Beatitudes as a handful of suggestions for better social living? His simple words were a clarion call to action and a profound statement of eventualities so revelatory to our mundane existence that we will have to experience them to understand.

The Redeemer of mankind made his bargain for us in joy and with anguish. He made a personal decision that could not be avoided if we were to be redeemed from death and the sins of flesh. He paid a terrible price, he came to be intimate with mortal death and divine resurrection, knowing his message would be largely unheard, ignored, rejected, even hated by the world. Are we, any of us today, living worthy of the price he paid? Are we seeking him, do we know the name by which we are called? Do we love and trust our Savior completely? Have you invited him into your heart and asked entrance into his rest?

I am reminded of the word often used to denote intimate relation-ships, it is the verb to cleave. This word had two meanings; one is to part along a natural line of division, as in the opposition of opinion and be-liefs. The other meaning is the reverse; to cling, adhere, remain faithful in spite of persecution or popularity. It is obvious that mankind has chosen to honor the former definition throughout world history, with the excep-tion of Jesus' ministry. Speaking of marriage to the ever wily Pharisees, Jesus taught that male and female were created to cleave together.

". . . For this cause shall a man leave father and mother, and shall cleave to his wife: and they twain shall be one flesh? Wherefore they are no more twain, but one flesh. What therefore God hath joined together, let not man put asunder." (Matthew 19:5-6).

We need to cleave unto Heavenly Father in this same way; that we can be of one spirit and one mind with Him. Our human need for love's nourishment is greater than our need for food. The world is filled with souls hungry for the bread of life. Men perish searching for the love that lives within them. The world is dying from a paucity of faith in the Master and his Kingdom. We can save the world with love and we can as committed Christians become saved from the world through our love, but it all must begin with our Father in Heaven. Let his love transform our heart, enhance and ennoble us. We can be as he is. We must ask if this is what we want for ourselves.

Only the kingdom of God offers hope and peace. It is to the sweet music of His eternal season that we must tune our instruments, quicken our rhythms in time with His. We must remember that to know our Father in Heaven and His Son, Jesus Christ is a transcending, revelatory experience — we are forever increased by it because it is the greatest experience we can know. Revelations are the proof of true religion. Through them, we his spirit children who dwell for a season in mortal vessels can know His desire that we live in loving harmony with each other and do not forget we are being prepared for future lives and responsibilities.

When we pass beyond this mortal veil, surely we will be interviewed by the Lord's angels who will report our answers to the Master: "What is it thou truly believes? What comes to thy mind as thou speaks of Jesus Christ? And again, What does thou believe with respect to the atonement of thy Savior and how has it figured in thy life on earth?"

Will we be as the Jews of old, not truly listening, rebelling of obedience? Or are we waiting upon the Lord for all things? In Mosiah King Benjamin tells his followers to keep the name of Christ written upon their hearts,

"For how knoweth a man the master whom he has not served, and who is a stranger unto him, and is far from the thoughts and intents of his heart?" (Mosiah 5:13)

How do we keep the name of God the Father written upon our hearts?

If we bond ourselves to Him in obedience, repentance, in trust and in fiercest love our spirit will be washed new in faith. Then we will be blessed to overflowing with divine guidance, forgiveness, personal healings and sudden insights. With divine love lighting our souls our pathway to the Tree of Life will become clear. Holding tightly to the rod of iron determination our journey will teach us discernment, courage and tolerance, patience, long suffering and selflessness based upon love that passes all understanding. That is the path to the Master and to our true home.

We have a lot to do. Today is the fifth year of an infant century. Let's go forward as emissaries of God, missionaries in His invincible army. Let's accept the challenge of our prophet to work at furthering the kingdom of God on earth. In this first step of our new thousand year journey let's work earnestly and busily to spread peace and love in the world, preach the gospel of the Father wherever we can. Let's commit to clearing the path for the Savior to walk upon at his return. I testify to you that if we will serve in that way, then the personal interrelationship with our Father in Heaven we are promised will be our joyous reward. In Doctrine and Covenants 128 the Prophet Joseph Smith received these thrilling words:

Brethren, shall we not go on in so great a cause? Go forward and not backward. Courage, brethren; and on, on to the victory! Let your hearts rejoice and be exceedingly glad. Let the earth break forth in singing . . . And let the sun, moon, and the morning stars sing together, and let all the sons of God shout for joy! . . . how glorious is the voice we hear from heaven, proclaiming in our ears, glory, and salvation, and honor, and immortality, and eternal life; kingdoms, principalities and powers! . . . Behold, the great day of the Lord is at hand . . . " (D&C 128: 22-24).

Believe the profoundly beautiful promises we faithful have each been offered. We are here for our own salvation, lest we forget. He who is perfect knows us in a personal and private way, as our parents or children can never know us. He has assured us "I will not leave you comfortless: I will come to you." (John 14:18)

Come to Heavenly Father naked of all fear and constraint, all pretense and pride. Lay before him your love, your gifts, your sin, your addictions, your fears, your hopes and dreams. Let him know you completely. Ask him to make you whole in him. Our Father in Heaven is our carpenter, the architect of our personalities, the author and finisher of our faith. His love is all transforming. For our God is a consuming fire. (Heb 12:29).

Religion is a personally transforming experience. Have you grown the faith to be transformed?

Renewed in Mother Eve:
Our Noble Legacy —

Shalom aleichem, my sisters, and *lashana tova tikusevu*, which means "may you be inscribed for a good year". I am honored to be among you this evening, this Jewish High Holy day, *Rosh Hashonah*. I hope that what we share here this evening will be pleasing and informative to you.

Are there any other Jews in the audience tonight? Any non-members? Single sisters? Remarried? I am or have been all of these. We are all sisters in the families of Israel and in the truest sense we are daughters both of our Heavenly parents and our first mortal parents.

I'm here tonight to share my conversion story with you. Not only my conversion to the Church, but my discovery that I am one of the daughters of Eve. That knowledge has literally remade me. Baptism in 1988 when I was almost to my 48th year of mortal life has impacted my character to a degree I never thought possible. Since baptism, the Holy Ghost has taught truths to my spirit. As a result, I've come to know myself as a spiritual woman.

I am grateful to be a Latter-day Saint, an inheritor of the wondrous mantle of our Mother Eve because we Latter-day Saint women are blessed with true principles to live by, ordinances and covenants to take upon ourselves, gifts we can develop which we may offer upon the altar of service to others in all seasons of our lives.

You know, this is the night of *Rosh Hashonah* which, for the Jewish world, means the head of the cycle" or "first of the year." According to Jewish belief it was on this day 5764 years ago that Adam was created and the world experienced the first *Rosh Hashonah*. *Rosh Hashonah* commemorates the birthday of the world and in a large sense looks toward fulfillment of peace and adjudication of all earthly problems. It is a time of rebirth through repentance. The Hebrew word here is "*teshuvah*" which means "to turn" from sin or error.

Regardless of how old the world really is, the eve of *Rosh Hashonah* begins the Ten Days of *teshuvah* (Days of Awe) that end in *Yom Kippur*, or Day of Atonement, services. On that day and night Jews are commanded to ask forgiveness of God for their accumulated sinfulness, but only after they have asked and received forgiveness from one another. During those 10 days the Jewish people ponder their acts towards others, how they have been, how they ought to be.

To the Latter-day Saint this date is also quite significant, for the Prophet Joseph Smith received the golden plates from the Angel Moroni on 22 September 1827, the day of *Rosh Hashonah*. Why was this significant? On this 'head of the cycle' day Jews all over the world were pleading with God to restore the covenant. And it happened, thus starting a new cycle in the lives of his ancient covenant people.

And so it can be with us here tonight — a reenergizing, a new vision for mind and heart. On this night we are invited to review our actions of 2003-4 and evaluate them. How do we measure up as disciples of Christ, as servants to our families and our community. Romans 8:16-17 teaches us that "the Spirit itself beareth witness with our spirit, that we are the children of God: and if children, then heirs; heirs of God, and joint-heirs with Christ."

Are we worthy daughters of our Heavenly Mother, of Mother Eve? We, like them, possess limitless potential. Our Relief Society motto "Charity Never Faileth" teaches us that showing kindness and compassion towards all with whom we come in contact blesses others as well as ourselves. We daily demonstrate that concern in our public professions or as wives and mothers, grandmothers, matriarchs. Tonight let us be a nucleus for new success as the fairer, gentler gender, and because ours are the hands that rock the cradles of the world, teach it, tend it, nurse and clean it, we sustain it. We are the Lord's best angels and perhaps this world's best hope for peaceful co-existence.

As for myself, I knew nothing of these concepts or of the Mormon people until I had lived nearly a half century. I had a very difficult time converting to this Church because of the Jewish mindset I grew up with. The conversion of Jews to the Church is still a rarity but increasingly they are accepting Jesus as their savior. In my case, I had reached the depths of despair because of my lifestyle, which was predicated upon age-old traditions and barriers. So, it took powerful experiences to bring me to Christ. Please bear with me. My story is an intensely personal one.

I must preface it by telling you that the history of the Hebrew people has been continuous for more than 5,000 years. They developed a unique religious system that has survived the onslaughts and conquests of twenty different nations and rulers, until in 1948 they became a Jewish nation again in Israel.

Judaism is a way of life embracing ethical and moral precepts covering every aspect of daily life, from hygiene and behavior to justice and equality before God and the law. It is a sub-civilization having territory, commerce, history, a culture, a social order, a unique identity, a language, philosophy and originally a race of people. It was the Semitic desert tribes and wandering Hebrews who brought these concepts together for the first time.

My heritage is Ashkenazic. These are the Jews who settled in Italy, France, Germany, Britain and eventually Eastern Europe. My father was born in 1910 in the little southwestern Ukrainian town of Berdichev, strategically important to the Nazis on their way into Russia in 1941.

I was very lucky to be born in America one year earlier than that, in Ohio. Initially, I was raised in a predominately Orthodox Jewish environment, progressing and regressing from a devout follower of Torah, which contain the first five books of what Christians call the Old Testament, to a somewhat Americanized observer of Jewish tradition. I am of the tribe of Judah. We have roots in Tsarist Russia. My mother's family comes from the Kiev area in Ukraine.

I grew up in a Jewish neighborhood in Los Angeles and I remember my first rabbi, his sweet charitable nature, his frizzy beard and his humorous acceptance of this Yiddishe *madele* (girl) who kept asking questions. Why doesn't God speak right to us, rabbi? Where is he, why can't I see him? Does he know me? Why do we hate Jesus? What happened to the prophets? Always I was asking questions, which is how a Jew encounters life. Of course, we continue to question the answers we receive. My rabbi never did answer those questions to my satisfaction.

My life was also tumultuous because of the severe family problems that continued throughout my teenaged years. My parents were usually at odds, they'd married in haste and soon regretted it. My parents' arguments and anger were often physical and none of us escaped it. By the time I was 17, I had become accustomed to my father's rage and his belt across my face on a regular basis. To this day I don't know why he resented me so, but from the time I was six or seven he told me I would never amount to anything. I needed and wanted my father to love me and if I had known the Gospel I would have petitioned my Father in Heaven to help me in my private trials, to protect me from my earthly father's rages and from my mother's displays of personal grief through her many suicide attempts.

God wasn't in our house, we always felt that our lives and home were cursed. But somehow the knowledge that I would one day escape my unhappy circumstances kept hope alive.

We belonged to a synagogue but as I became a teenager my folks were divorced and fell away from it, though Mother and I continued on a very irregular basis. So there was little spiritual growth or participation for us as a family or as individuals.

How did all of this affect me? I was the first born by seven years, but because I was not born a boy I was usually on the discount table. I always seemed to be disappointing my parents, and when my brother, their first and only son, was born, it was as if their true desires had finally been met. I felt deeply disliked, cast aside and taken for granted. My mother was a nurse and often worked long hours, so I was recruited in my preteens to clean the house and make dinner for my father and brother most every night. I became a cook and housekeeper long before I knew anything else and that has pretty much continued. I was never treated with any particular interest by my parents. To many Jewish households, if the first born is not a male, the family believes it is cursed.

When I was 14, I was confirmed from Hebrew Sunday School, but I decided to leave the synagogue altogether because I felt no happiness there. I took this up with my mother. She did not understand my concerns. She cried that I was unfaithful, she cursed and threatened me but I cried back

"Something is missing! I don't feel that God is with me in the synagogue. There's more to this, there has to be!"

Mother was a true believer in Judaism.

"Can a rabbi be wrong?" she asked. "God hears your prayers but we have to pray as a people, not only for ourselves."

All I could say was "I don't know, but this isn't right, this isn't enough, something's missing, I need more."

I vowed then to find the missing part if it took all of my life. My parents eventually divorced. But I was still unhappy. Eventually I found myself looking for love in all the wrong places. Several times I narrowly escaped death at the hands of evil people. My father in his visits continually called me a failure and said I would become a fallen woman (though I never fulfilled his expectations). My mother didn't bother to defend me. The effect all this had on me is that I seriously questioned the value of living a life bereft of self-esteem, family cohesiveness or parental approval. By the end of my 30's I'd learned a lot of the world's uglier lessons first hand and experienced several personal tragedies that devastated me and which almost convinced me that life in general was fruitless. I felt I would always be alone, that no man would think I was worthy of caring for.

My mother eventually disowned both her children, choosing instead to disappear with all the family pictures and mementos. She was never seen or heard of by any of us again. I searched for her many years. My own dreams of husband and family never materialized. I married early but divorced several years later. As time went on, I began to think about painless ways of ending my seemingly fruitless existence.

If I had known my essential worth as a child of God and that I have a Heavenly Mother and an enduring example of heroic Eve, as LDS women are taught, I could have been saved from many of the mistakes I made that were caused by a poor and potentially disastrous view of myself, my posterity, my family and my God.

Let us stop here for a moment and consider the woman Eve while still in the Garden. Eve's Hebrew name is pronounced *khav vav*, meaning "life giver" with a further description of her calling, *am khol chay* in Hebrew, meaning "mother of all living" or "mother of all life."

Isn't that an unimaginable task? What was she like? We do know she was the prime example of a deeply spiritual, courageous and noble woman. Yet popular media for years has pictured her as some weak-willed figure. Even the Washington Post years ago referred to her story in the book of Genesis as having a more profoundly negative impact on women throughout history than any other biblical story. Recently the news media featured an article on Turkish women. It reported they are routinely beaten and denied any voice in the lives of their family and community. The Turkish government enforces their bondage. This is not good news for the daughters of Eve.

It is true that legally and socially, civilizations have adopted this erroneous and misunderstood story of Eve to fit their concepts of who women are and are not and how they should be treated, or that should read mis-treated. Various religions have used Eve's role in the Fall as a rationale for canon law and ecclesiastical positioning. My own father, who was taught better by his Jewish mother, came to view women as foolish, inherently evil and ultimately not worth his bother. I, of course, learned to see myself in the same way and for a number of years acted accordingly.

What's wrong with this picture? What we must not forget is that we have inalienable worth. What does inalienable mean? It means God-given, that which mankind can not take from us. We are each of us inheritors of the legacy of Eve.

Let's discuss for a few moments what that legacy is.

Elder Bruce R. McConkie has written extensively about the role Mother Eve plays in the lives of women today. I quote:

"There is no language that can do credit to our glorious mother, Eve. Eve — a daughter of God, one of the spirit offspring of the Almighty Elohim — was among the noble and great in (pre-mortal) existence. She ranked in spiritual stature, in faith and devotion, in conformity to eternal law with Michael".

We know Michael to be Adam, a prince and the patriarch of the human family.

These are amazing words. Women have for centuries sold themselves short of mortal or eternal value. In America until recently we couldn't vote. The women's rights movement a few years back was an attempt to revolutionize that destructive pattern. It is only recently that legislation was written giving us equal rights with men, but equal pay is still a few eons away.

But in our temples we are taught that our beloved Mother Eve was long-suffering and heroic. So understanding Eve's real role is vital to our realizing our true worth because that can make all the difference.

Picture this: Adam and Eve are together in a beautiful garden. Lucifer finds Adam alone and tries to convince him to sin and fails. He then finds Eve alone and holds out the importance of knowing good and evil to her. She with spiritual perception and intuitive wisdom sees, beyond the blandishments of the tempter, the importance of the commandment that they multiply and replenish the earth. Somehow she understands the mighty importance of that instruction. The world sees Eve as a primary instigator. Her firstborn was Cain.

But, in Alma 12:22, 31 Alma explained that by Adam's fall . . . they learned good from evil. In short, they became free to have a family, free to learn to truly love, free to act according to their wills, whether to yield to the plan of God or subject themselves to the devil, free to enjoy the fruits of the plan of redemption, the plan of mercy, the plan of happiness, free to choose and to be accountable. Eve did the right thing, made the right choice, had the intuitive comprehension to see the end from the beginning. Eve made a noble choice. We honor her. She was spiritually mature.

Eve learned first that knowledge meant loss of innocence and that it carried a heavy price. Remaining in the Garden was impossible. She and Adam could never progress, they could never be parents or be free to use their agency to discover their inherent potential.

Eve was heroic. She was able to see the great possibilities and promises that awaited all of mankind through hers and Adam's sacrifice. She found that, associated with the penalties of mortality there were also untold blessings in store. What were the blessings? The Plan of Salvation as Heavenly Father explained it to them in conjunction with the atonement. Eve and Adam immediately agreed to it.

And so Eve endured bravely with her husband their metamorphosis from a celestial life to a mortal one where evil as well as good abounded. Their lives were surely filled with hardship, enduring the elements, hunger, the attendant pains of childbirth, fatigue, age, and mortal death.

Yet Mother Eve brought forth the human family with gladness and charity, loving and teaching her children, grateful for the challenges they would bring to her. She was willing to assume the problems connected with a family, but also the joys. She was active in the planning and preparation that has shaped our sphere and our mortality. Now it is true that we are in a mortal world where disappointment, sorrow for sin, etc. are also present, but any success and glory we can have owes its beginnings to Eve's example. And that legacy has been passed on to all of womanhood. It is a glorious legacy. We each have a mighty errand to do. It may or may not include marriage and motherhood at this time, but ours is the errand of influence.

That got me thinking about our Heavenly Mother, our eternal mother. With these examples always before us, we do not have to succeed by the world's standards because when we follow the Lord's admonitions we cannot fail to find happiness and success in even the smallest ways. He supports us in these endeavors.

How I wish my parents and I had known of this special legacy that women are heir to. Let's keep these things in mind as I continue my story.

In my 41st year my brother Mark drove from his home in San Jose to San Diego to bring me a Book of Mormon. He had married a Tongan woman in the mid-70's and eventually converted to the Church. He said

"Sis, you need Christ in your life", to which I replied:

"I don't need Christ in my life, I am a Jew, we don't believe Jesus is the Messiah."

I already had a Torah. I put the Book of Mormon away in the bookcase and forgot about it. That book found a home on various bookshelves and in packing boxes for nine hard, lonely and financially poor years while I continued to falter in my search for meaning and purpose, working hard but earning little, I enrolled myself as a charter member of the Failures of America club.

Now, as a Jewish woman I had been taught that women are to be loved, served, even revered by our husband and children. We are the heart of a home, the essence of the home. That value is inherent in Jewish culture. But I was divorced. I had grown up in a home where Jewish values were largely thrown by the wayside. The only culture I knew was one of self-denial, self-dislike, hard work with no vacations or a family to spend them with, and general abandonment of all noble values. Instead I believed the common societal views. Unfortunately, millions of women worldwide still hold to the untruth that we are inherently sinful, of less value than men and that we need to somehow apologize for our gender, as though there is something not quite right about it. Hold that thought.

Back to the conversion process:

Eventually missionaries visited me on Mark's referral; but after the second discussion and a visit to the Mormon Battalion church in San Diego, I sent them away. In the First Discussion they told me that Jehovah of the Old Covenant and the Hebrew Torah was Jesus Christ, the living Son of the living God, their Savior and mine. I had never heard that. I didn't accept it. Jews believe Jehovah is Heavenly Father as well as the God of Israel. Here were some so-called latter day Hebrews telling me that God does not operate alone and that the Messiah of the Jews is Jesus Christ, co-creator with God of this world and that Jesus is the God of Israel. They spoke to me as though I had a mind of my own. They never talked down to me. They told me I was a daughter of God. I was speechless.

From a religious point of view, to a Jew, the name of *Yeshua*, the enlightened, is the bringer of freedom through spiritual light, a teacher, a rabbi. Here were Christian missionaries calling *Yeshua* the Christ. I could not understand that. To bring the name of Jesus into a Jewish home usually sets off total resistance, ostracism, perhaps even hatred, fear and possible alienation from family members far and wide. I was afraid to believe the wonderful things I was hearing. *Yeshua* means wide open, free, hence freedom, liberty, redemption, salvation etc. It also means the one who brings this condition about, hence Savior, Redeemer, Liberator, etc.

The missionaries told me of the Grand Council in Heaven and said that everyone on the earth was at that meeting where Jesus was chosen to be the only begotten Son of God, that he was and is the Christ, as well as the Jewish *Mashiach*, or Messiah. It all sounded strange and wonderful, but I was unable to accept it because Jews believe very differently.

The missionaries also said I had a mother in Heaven. They believed I had a distinct and personal reason for being on the earth at this time and that I was given many talents to use in forging a life for myself. They told me I was an inheritor of the legacy of Mother Eve.

Goodness! All these mothers! These were things my earth mother had never told me. I found myself examining my behavior and thinking I should be reevaluating myself in the light of these revelations because I was aware that I did not measure up to the examples that were put before me.

But I could not allow the missionaries to continue. I hated even the thought that any Jew would actually accept Jesus as the Savior. Jews do not believe anyone has yet been resurrected or come to earth as a Messiah. But I was afraid to believe these things, and also afraid of the changes in myself and my lifestyle they would require.

So, in my wisdom, I sent the missionaries away. I was not ready to live a chaste lifestyle. I did not care for the image of Mother Eve that I was presented with. I was working for little pay while attending an expensive college on a state loan and worrying about finances, so I certainly did not want to pay a tithe, although Jews are taught to tithe. In short, I was a worldly woman. Humility and obedience were not my best qualities. I was proud of being a free spirit. I didn't realize I was in a cage of my own making.

But a tiny seed had been planted. It bore strange fruit at first. As I passed an LDS chapel on my way to synagogue, I began to wonder if those missionaries were right when they told me I had a personal Savior who knew and loved me.

So, against all better judgment I began a strange and secret liaison. On the following Friday night I attended services at my synagogue and on Sunday I drove to an LDS chapel. I waited until its congregation left, because I thought they would know I was Jewish and tell me to leave. Stealing inside, I made myself sit there, in a church, and pray. Always, I made sure I was alone and undiscovered. My first prayer was for forgiveness for entering a church with a plea attached that I would not be struck dead on the spot.

When I felt safe and undisturbed I prayed for relief from many problems. I could feel a strong, human presence behind me. Somehow I knew I was being listened to. I knew something was there, but I saw no one. I heard only my shaky voice. It was mystifying and new and very energizing. Even more mystifying was that during the following week all my prayers were answered. It amazed me so much I went to that chapel numerous times on Sundays after Friday night synagogue services. I told God all my temporal and spiritual problems. These prayers were always answered, sometimes within a day. It was a revelation that I could be heard on a personal level and that my requests were actually answered. I felt so peaceful and comforted. Maybe this was what I told my mother was missing from synagogue services.

My life quickly improved. I found a mechanic for my car, all the little problems I had were resolved quickly, old friends called and visited, and it seemed I was filled with a spirit of peace. I made sure to go to synagogue also, just to keep things evened out.

Eventually all my prayers were answered, so I stopped my secret forays into the chapels. But I never forgot what were to me miraculous blessings. It was a completely different feeling from synagogue attendance and very satisfying to my spirit.

Let's reflect again. What was I learning at this point? I was pondering on a subconscious level what the missionaries had taught me. I am a child of God. I carry a holy spirit. I was planned for, I entered mortality on purpose and I am here to progress and to be tested as to my worthiness. I was not meant to fail but to succeed. But my success was not really measurable by the world's screwy standards. This eventually made a walloping big difference in my attitude toward myself and my outlook on life.

I also learned that Jesus of Nazareth, a Jew, atoned with his life for my sins. That made me responsible for my actions and gave me the very guilty feeling that I owed God for the mistakes and sins I had made in my life. I didn't like that feeling.

And I was beginning to realize, that like Eve I had chosen to learn things that tempted and tried me. But whereas she saw the positive, eternal possibilities in the consequences of her choices, I thought that my lifestyle was the only way for me to live because I didn't feel worthy of more. There was also the problem that I did not know how to ask for God's help to change.

So I stepped backward into my Garden of Disorder, to reevaluate and reassess my personal tree of knowledge of good and evil. Pruning was in order. When I'd ventured into the world in my teens I thought I was being wise, I thought my lifestyle was good food, and I partook unwisely. My garden snake was my own errant will and I let it seduce me from the garden of innocence to the lone and dreary world of sinfulness and sorrow.

By 1985, I had almost forgotten my experiences with prayer in LDS chapels. I moved to Oregon to be near my brother's family when his wife died of cancer at 34, leaving four small children to be raised. Immediately, his neighbors, stake missionaries, began visiting me, Over my loud objections to Christianity in any dress, they assured me I wouldn't have to give up anything, but only add to what I already understood. I said I wasn't going to be seduced into believing a modern prophet existed or that Jesus was the Mashiach and I still wouldn't allow myself to attend their church meetings. I had been taught to honor my heritage and was not about to embrace Christianity just because I'd had those peaceful, wonderful experiences in the San Diego chapels.

That year my father was found dead in his store in California. He was for a long time a victim of severe depression and he had isolated himself from the world several years before his death, turning his children away. I would love to have cared for him or at the very least to have said good-bye to him and receive his blessing. I loved my father more than anyone I have ever known. But he never wanted my love nor would he give of himself to anyone. I was informed of his death by a business associate.

Following my father's funeral I was deeply depressed. The stake missionaries met me with open arms, which I skillfully dodged. But they kept tabs on me. They were excited to tell me about the Restoration of the original teachings of Jesus Christ, as the first missionaries had done. They said members of The Church of Jesus Christ of Latter-day Saints were also partakers of the blessings of the Abrahamic Covenant between God and the Jewish people, that the LDS were of the original twelve Hebrew tribes. The missionaries kept knocking at my door. They said animal sacrifices were no longer necessary because the atonement of Jesus Christ was an infinite atonement, sufficient for all people and for all time. They assured me that Jesus came to earth as a Jewish man, that he WAS and IS the Messiah.

I assured them I was not interested in my eternal possibilities or in someday meeting my maker. I refused to consider their words, but I could not forget the happy look in their eyes as they spoke, or the knots of emotion that rose within me. I fought it as hard as I could, but something kept at me, beckoning, whispering. These new ideas were becoming a real problem that needed solving. For months I pondered their words, but I was stubborn and would not pray about it as they urged me to do. The dark old ways were comfy and familiar.

But the Spirit beckoned. Eventually I made a deal with the stake missionaries when they moved to an old farm house. I offered to help them pay for and build a room onto their dilapidated barn. There I moved in among the goats, the chickens and the mice, the horse and cow and other barnyard citizens. I vowed not to leave until I had fully investigated their scriptures and my own and come to a definite conclusion about the falsity of their claims.

That Oregon winter was a miserable one, but I hung in there for five-and-a-half months, in that cold room with no heat or facilities other than a bare bulb. I was 47, with no job, no money, no husband or children, no direction and much confusion about the purpose of my life. I had nothing to lose, I had to solve the puzzle all these missionaries were giving me. Where did I really come from? Why was I here, where was I going? Why did they care so much what I believed? Why couldn't I persuade myself they were all wrong?

Every woman is special, a somebody of intrinsic worth who has been a somebody for a very long time, indeed, forever. Every daughter of God, born of divine heritage in the spirit before this world was formed, enters mortality already a special, eternal person. Each has proved herself in demanding periods of trial, has chosen the right course and pursued it with faith and courage, and comes here with credentials earned in pre-mortal worlds.

President Spencer W. Kimball has counseled,

"The world is increasing in wickedness. Temptations are greater than they have ever been in the memory of any of us. In the face of these conditions — and they will get worse. We must ever keep in mind that it is the design of Satan to thwart the plan of our Eternal Father. Before the world was created, in heavenly councils the pattern and role of women were prescribed. You women were elected by God to be wives and mothers in Zion, priestesses to your husbands, and eventually gods yourselves."

Well, I didn't hear that talk by President Kimball or any other prophet or apostle, nor was I a mother in any setting, so I had a whole different and far less desirable idea of my purpose in life. But when I entered that cocoon of a room in October of 1987, I entered as a woman with a noble heritage of another kind, with five centuries of incalculable Hebraic history at my back. Many times I imagined choice curses were being hurled at me by a billion Jewish voices who had gladly paid with their lives to retain their Jewish identity.

That first step was as if an imaginary threshold had been built for me to enter, which I did with much trepidation and misgiving. I had lost all my childhood illusions by then. My long and short term goal at that point was to keep breathing. But there I was, stepping out of my comfort zone as a Jewish woman with a specific and familiar identity. I'd never thought to question that more knowledge would better define me as a soul with unknown and unexplored potential — but it was at that low point of my life, which the Lord knew I had reached, that the road not taken became the path to enlightenment.

I took with me the sacred books of both religions. These I spread out on my single bunk.

Over a five-and-a-half month period in that cold room I read through centuries of the Lord's words, his blessings and penalties, his interventions in the lives of his children, first the Old Covenant, specifically the prophets, with Isaiah as the central cog of the ancient prophetic wheel. As a teenager I loved the words of Isaiah. Now rereading them as if for the first time I read in chapter 43 of the eventual deliverance of Israel, the promise of their release from exile, one of Isaiah's favorite themes. The

Lord speaks through this great prophet and tells all of Israel that after she is driven to all corners of the earth she will be gathered again.

As the hours became months, I learned again the Plan of Salvation, our pre-mortal life, the Grand Council in Heaven, the Fall of Lucifer, our first parents Adam and Eve. I read for the first time of Eve's mission and her great courage. Jews know nothing of the Fall or the lessons that can be learned from it. I was finding a role model who could uplift me and speak to me about my own worth and purpose in mortality. These scriptures rang in me a bell of awakening and of gladness and I many times dropped to my knees for verification of these great happenings. But that witness was held from me. I knew I was on the hardest, longest path of my life and that any further life I could have depended on my finishing what I had started.

What new lessons was I learning?

I am a worthwhile person and woman because I am a daughter of Heavenly Father and I have come to this world because of my faithfulness in the pre-mortal worlds. I am not a failure, but a soul seeking truth.

I was discovering that the Gospel of Jesus Christ was an essential tool in my life, an implement to discover and develop my self worth. President Lorenzo Snow once counseled:

"Though Christ a thousand times in Bethlehem be born, If he is not born in thee, thy soul is still forlorn."

My biological father did not have any understanding of my true worth or of my mother's worth as a woman, nor did my mother know how valuable a person she intrinsically was.

I had been selling myself short in my life goals, which were extremely unsure by that time in my life. I could have a new life and a new beginning, a God-directed life.

Becoming worthy was first in importance, then finding a worthy mate, one who held the priesthood of God, was next. I might not be able to have children in this world, but there were promises that in other worlds I would be able to raise them with my eternal companion.

A good marriage with eternal possibilities was what I should be striving for after I had done the work necessary to be worthy of a lasting marriage. That was becoming the plan.

What was the foundation of all this new understanding? It was the news that Jesus is the Holy One of Israel, Jehovah, personal savior and the savior of mankind, the *Mashiach*. *Yeshua*, the name of salvation, prosperity, deliverance, freedom and victory. He was not just another preacher in Jerusalem. He was not a fake Messiah, but he is the Messiah of the world, he is the name of freedom and deliverance from bondage of all kinds. He is not dead, he lives and he has promised to return to the Jewish people, he will persuade them this time that he is and has always been their long-awaited *Mashiach*. His sacrifice was made in his atonement. Jesus, Yeshua, is the miracle.

My heart leapt within me. My God, I prayed, in awe of worlds opening to me, how can this be? I could not stop, not to eat, not to argue, not to do anything. I sat on that bed whole days and feasted upon the words of Christ and thought about myself as a woman with value, promise, a life outside the barn.

What else was I learning? The Doctrine & Covenants immediately wrote itself into my heart. It reminded me of the Talmud corrected and edited!

I knew it was scripture, pure and exact. I learned there are ordinances necessary for salvation and exaltation. Jewish canon does not prepare anyone for exaltation so we blind souls are like rats in a trap. No saving ordinances of any kind exist in Judaism.

I had stepped into mortality with my eyes opened but somewhere along the way there were blinders limiting my sight. Now I was learning that I had a kind and loving Heavenly Father who was eager for me to know him and to accept His Son and the atonement.

I was also learning that I liked myself this new way. I had worth that didn't come from the approval of a boyfriend or the look of a new dress or any other physical reality. It came from inside myself, based upon my new knowledge of my first, true heritage as a child of God and an inheritor of the nobility and courage of Mother Eve.

Elder Orson F. Whitney described the Fall as having a two-fold direction — downward, yet forward. It brought mankind into the world and set his feet upon progression's highway.

Well, I had already gone downward. In fact, I was so far down I couldn't see up. I had looked to the world for answers but found only empty pleasures.

Finally I had to grapple with the fundamental truth of all. If the Book of Mormon and the Doctrine and Covenants are true books, then The Church of Jesus Christ of Latter-day Saints is the true Church restored because Joseph.Smith was a modern prophet, and all that the missionaries had been telling me throughout those years of intense searching, is true. The restored gospel does provide all that is needed for exaltation whereas synagogues deal only with mortality. Temples have once again been erected, ordinances that pertain to eternal life have been restored, and this is the time of the restoration of all things. And my life was not in vain, it had all been in preparation for the future I could have. It was the sentence I was soon to receive that put the cap on everything.

Could I finally accept the fact that long ago in Palestine there was a man, a Jew who came to teach the Kingdom of God to those from whose loins we are all descended? That he, finishing the Last Hebrew Passover with his disciples, walked from that table to the Garden of Gethsemane to begin his infinite atonement. What he did there split history down the middle and echoes throughout eternities. Now, finally I was able to read of this and contemplate the great love our Savior has for each soul who would ever live. I pondered that many, many days and nights. How could any mortal give up his life to God so that no further sacrifices would ever have to be made, then rise from his grave as if death had no claim on him? This Jesus they wrote of, he must have been an immortal being. It must all be true . . .

I had walked inside that musty room a natural woman. I emerged happier, full of the light of understanding, with faith and especially with hope. The scriptures had nurtured a healthier, spiritually alive "me" with a sincere determination to go the rest of the way.

One glorious day soon afterward I was standing outside the barn when a miracle occurred. A voice spoke to me. It was a heavenly presence, real as myself there next to me. I saw and heard him. He knew it was time, I was ready. He was truly present as a being. I saw and felt his weight and presence. He gave me one sentence: "It's all in how you think about it."

It was like the truth came at once into my soul! I was filled with joy, with a sudden understanding that I was now truly free to believe whatever I chose. As I stood there I began vibrating from my toes to my head, filling with light, filling with joy, for the first time, knowing that all of it, everything I had read, everything the missionaries had told me is true. My heart pounded, I felt I was growing a new one to fill up new space. At one point the pressure was so great I thought I would burst open.

Then, all at once I knew that this is Heavenly Father's Church. He has a Son who came into the world to save it and he gave his precious life for us in that terrible act upon the cross. Best of all is that he lives. He is Jesus Christ and he is the Jewish *Mashiach*, our Redeemer, our Advocate with the Father, he is our Intercessor who will plead in our behalf. He is our friend, our compatriot, our heart's desire, our comforter, our Creator, our everything.

Why, then, was I born a Jew? To experience some of the progression and passion of biblical history. To learn that truth is a tapestry of revelations, faith, obedience, repentance, hope. The Old Covenant is not old, the New not new, Book of Mormon not newer, they are all part of one fluid, moving long record.

I was baptized April 6, 1988. In the confirmation prayer I was told my purpose in this life. It is to be a missionary for Christ. The Holy Ghost has testified to me that my mission is to be an Esther to my people through my books, firesides and personal missionary work. I had lived almost a half-century before learning my purpose.

Three years ago I married a man in the Church and we are, after a lot of getting accustomed to each other in our hoary old years, even happy together. In my long and lonely life, in and out of unhappy circumstances, childless and with little hope of finding fulfillment, I have learned more of my true worth and the urgent need to grow in worthiness. I have seen that the prophets of this Church speak the truth with wisdom and foresight that comes of their seership as mouthpieces for the very God of us all. I look also to them for my spiritual well being.

Recently, I listened to our Prophet's wife, our dear and very recently departed Sister Margery Hinckley, who gave testimony of her thoughts on motherhood in a 2003 fireside for women. She said:

"I don't want to drive up to the pearly gates in a shiny sports car, wearing beautifully, tailored clothes, my hair expertly coiffed, and with long, perfectly manicured fingernails.

"I want to be there with a smudge of peanut butter on my shirt from making sandwiches for a sick neighbor's children.

"I want to be there with a little dirt under my fingernails from helping to weed someone's garden.

"I want to be there with children's sticky kisses on my cheeks and the tears of a friend on my shoulder.

"I want the Lord to know I was really here and that I really lived."

In our temple endowment session Latter-day Saint women are reminded that Eve's calling as the "mother of all living" was conferred upon her by Heavenly Father. She understood her mission while still in the Garden and she played a significant and courageous role in the Fall. She exercised her agency to accept a life outside the confines of Heavenly paradise and strove with Adam to attain the privilege of returning to God. How did she do that? By remaining faithful in her God-given roles. She was a devoted wife to her husband and a loving, dedicated mother to her many children. She gave her life to the lives of others. Mother to the mortals to come. So what can we immediately learn from this?

In The Pearl of Great Price, in Moses, chapter five we find:

Our first mortal mother was a noble, forward looking, successful woman in her own right. As she lived she grew in understanding and wisdom. She carried the mantle she had been given with honor.

Eve knew how and when to exercise her agency because she acted in concert with the Plan of her Father in Heaven.

Eve kept her covenant with Heavenly Father to hearken to her husband as he hearkened unto God.

She was a woman who worked side by side with her husband. They reigned together, they fell together, they toiled in the world outside the Garden together, raising and teaching their many children to live righteously.

Eve understood, accepted and magnified her role as companion to Adam. They acted together, in unity with the knowledge of their eternal worth as separate souls and as an eternal family.

She never fell to Evil, for her eyes had been opened and she knew evil from good. She used her agency for the good of all concerned.

We have the same opportunities, the same trials, the same legacy to pass on to our sons and daughters, our grandchildren and great grandchildren.

Let's discuss that a moment. The Prophet Joseph Smith had an understanding of who Eve had become. In a vision he related: "The heavens gradually opened and they saw a golden throne, on a circular foundation, something like a lighthouse, and on the throne were two aged personages, having white hair, and clothed in white garments. They were the two most beautiful and perfect specimens of mankind he ever saw.

Joseph said, 'They are our first parents, Adam and Eve.'"

What does this vision tell us? They tell us much of the rightness of Eve's actions and the acceptability of her contribution. The Prophet's vision was of Eve after her life on earth. She had fulfilled her important assignment gloriously.

Before the world was created, in heavenly councils the pattern and role of women were prescribed. You sisters were elected by God to be wives and mothers in Zion. Exaltation in the celestial kingdom is predicated on faithfulness to that calling.

Since the beginning, a woman's first and most important role has been ushering into mortality spirit sons and daughters of our Father in Heaven.

Since the beginning, her role has been to teach her children eternal gospel principles. She is to provide for her children a haven of security and love-regardless of how modest her circumstances might be.

How many of you are mothers? How many are waiting to become mothers? How many of you are like me, no children of our own but have helped rear and counsel the children including daughters of others? This message is for all of us. When Adam, his eyes now opened, blessed God and thanked Him that they should again be in His presence,

Eve heard all these things and was glad, saying — and now comes a perfect one-sentence summary of the whole plan of salvation, (Moses 5:11), one of the greatest short sermons ever preached:

Eve says, "Were it not for our transgression we never should have had seed, and never should have known good and evil, and the joy of our redemption, and the eternal life which God giveth unto all the obedient."

Thus, in the beginning, the perfect pattern is set for perfecting the family. The man and the woman are together in worship; they are together in teaching their children; they are together in establishing the family unit that hopefully will endure in the eternities ahead, thus giving eternal life to all those who earn it.

One of the most stirring success stories in scripture is told in the Book of Mormon of Lamanite women who taught their sons the gospel in the home. These two thousand sixty (2,060) young men were taught faith in God at their mothers' knees. Later, they exhibited great faith and courage when they went to war.

In Alma 56:47 their leader, Helaman, said of them, "Yea, they had been taught by their mothers, that if they did not doubt, God would deliver them." There is the key — "they had been taught by their mothers"!

Sisters, continue to give love's nourishment to everyone you can in the spirit of Eve. Why? Our need of love is greater than our need for food. Support, encourage, and strengthen your husband in his responsibility as patriarch in the home. You are partners with him. A woman's role in a man's life is to lift him, to help him uphold lofty standards, and to prepare through righteous living to be his queen for all eternity.

The world is filled with souls hungry for the bread of life. People perish searching for the love that lives within them. The world is dying from a paucity of faith in the Master and his Kingdom. We as women and sisters with the glorious calling of mothers in Zion can save the world with love and we can as committed Saints be saved from the world through our love, but it all must begin with individual commitment to Jesus Christ and the principles of eternal life.

Why? Because the seasons of mortal life are only short prologue to the seasons of eternal life. Whatever time we have here is short compared to the work we can do to further the Kingdom of God. What choice spirits we are to be reserved as wives and mothers in Zion at this critical hour!

And now, I will officially declare it *Rosh Hashonah* with the blowing of the shofar, the ram's horn, which Jewish people blow on this night to call everyone to repentance, renewal and rejoicing. There is order to the nature, sequence and frequency of the blasts blown from the smaller end of the horn, which is not supposed to be altered in any way. Rabbis developed elaborate rules that state broken notes should resemble sobbing, that a long unbroken note must precede and follow the broken ones. Many Jews speculate the Advent of their *Mashiach* will be heralded by the sound of a *shofar* and that God will use the *shofar* to deliver the trump sound of the Advent of the *Mashiach*.

[BLOW THE SHOFAR]

I testify to you, dear sisters, the truthfulness and eternal nature of your honored place as women, as caretakers in and of our homes and in our world. I testify to you that the Gospel of Jesus Christ, has been restored to the earth for all to know and live. Tonight let us renew our resolve to live nobler and richer lives as Saints in the Zion of this lovely valley, to be stronger, happier and more proactive than we have ever been. Let us attach the name "Eve" to our own. Let her live in us and let us rise to the glory that awaits us, I pray in the sacred name of Jesus Christ, amen.

This essay was first presented in March 2004. It makes an ideal fireside for September use because that is the time of Rosh Hashanah.

© *2004 by Marlena Tanya Muchnick*

Recognition and thanks to Beverly Campbell, past Director of International Affairs for The Church of Jesus Christ of Latter-day Saints. Her seminal address on Mother Eve was given April 2, 1993, at the 11th annual Conference of Collegium Aesculapium, Salt Lake City, Utah.

LATTER-DAY PSALMS

A Child's Rhyme —

(for Meredith)

"What is love?" one asked of me.
It comes of God. It's charity.
"And what is that?" one asked again.
I pondered more and answered then:

Love is the joy our Savior feels for all his flock.
Love's eternal — it minds no clock.

When we lived as spirit children,
Our Father taught us all
To know His ways so we'd progress
In doing deeds of happiness.

To kindly think, to gently touch.
I'm thankful that we learned so much!
He taught that giving of our time
And talents is a task divine
That brings relief to those who pine
For God's great care.

Jesus lives to love us all.
We are his greatest hope.
Though we will have our trials in life
He's taught us how to cope:

Let love for God unite all souls
In brotherhood and peace.
Be faithful, sweet and giving, dear.
Then watch your worries cease.

Love is the engine of the worlds
Bringing hope in time of strife.
Open your heart to all. Enjoy
The miracle that is life.

A Song of Renewal —

I think a seed hears that beat of time
Shuddering it toward life, its nascent memory stirs
A prescient song that God,
exulting in His creations,
Wrought upon it.

How must it feel?
That shivering readiness to be touched
By Majesty.

I would awake like the tocsin of cymbals and drums
Wonder at tremors lifting me
Rolling and twisting.
Molded like fire gorges sand
A hot, surging chrysalis of glowing glass
Until I am pliant,
Eager for the Craftsman's tongs.

I think there is a Muse of seed life,
Trumpets rally forth upon shards of air,
Herald each renewal as found treasure
And symphonies accompany
The solemn unfolding of a flower.

See the universe as a perpetual foundry of God
Who ignites the forge that illumines life.
It is like a song of love;
His everlasting lullaby
Of eternal rebirth.

Song Of Inspiration —

My Father, Whom I love so dear,
Thou art my Light, my shining hour.
Beneath Thy just, refining[1] Hand
My blessings multiply.

As Thou reveals Thy will, Thy Law[2] —
This student lists, on bended knee,
With quickened ear and grateful heart.
And knows that Thou art God of all.

O bring me joy and whisper nigh
Thy secrets of eternity
That I may hear Thy deepest thoughts,
That truth may ever burn in me[3].

O loose me not, my precious Lord
For I, thy child am evermore
Thy servant, thy disciple suffering long.
But bless me as the Saints[4] of old:
Smart and brave and gospel strong

That I may more fully serve Thee On High
In this waste place,
Then later in Thy courts of Peace.

O, how I love Thee, Father.
Father, how I love Thy Son.
Who ransomed[5] me from death and from
The awful sins of flesh

That I might come forth to see Thee,
To dwell forever in Thy Light.

---

[1] 2 Ne 24:2
[2] D&C 19:26; 84:44
[3] Heb 12:29; D&C 84:44
[4] D&C 45:45; 84:2
[5] Matt 20:28; D&C 95:1, D&C 56:18

Song of Charity —

Now, a poem most sweetly given.
Spirit, lift my thoughts to heaven,
To those happy courts above
Where angels sing most sacred songs
Of astounding love.

What is it that defeats the gloom?
Bringing gladness ere we roam?
The noise and vapors of our deeds.
The help we give to those in need
Flows upward to our heaven's home. [1]

Becomes the measure of our room,
Our mansions, our eternities.

And when we love as we are loved,
by One who endured all sacrifice
When we serve at any price
The perfect One whose name we claim
Charity becomes our Name. [2]

What treasure lives within our bones,
White as salt but little known?
Why whiteness built into our frames? [3]
The message — give and want no more.
We are the salt whereof Jesus spoke
"Let it pour. Let it pour." [4]

And when we love as we are loved,
by One who endured all sacrifice
When we serve at any price
The perfect One whose name we claim
Charity becomes our Name.

But where is our Deliverer?
Our brother, father, friend, our all?

Song of Redeeming Love —

Heavenly Father,
Thou with whom seraphs [1] abide,
Come, lift our spirits with Thy flame of lasting love,
Thy perfect grace.
That all who enter in Thy care
May see again [2]
Thy sacred Face.

O, may our souls be giv'n unto
Eternal joy and peace.
Thy grace abounds. Thy mercy swells
The hearts of all who hear Thy call.

The sweetest melody of all.
Thy wondrous song of redeeming love [3].

---

[1] *2 Ne 16:2; Isa 6:2*

[2] *Abr 3:22-26*

[3] *Mormon 9:12; Moses 5:11; D&C 138*

Artifacts —

It was the first clear day in June
When I quit the old city
And ran away to the sea,
Seeking to excavate my time remaining
Form the routines and façades
Of daily course — mere hollowed out sounds.

I drove time-cracked roads brittle as ancient crockery
Not roads but stratum collaged;
Cement and broken shell
Bits of fossil dredged up from vanished seas
Spread out again like pigment across the crust of lands
Everywhere.

What history beneath our feet!
Biblical coelecanths, flat shelled ammonites,
Snails, timeless and snug in golden spirals,
Magical seaworms touched somehow with light
Twisting through mazes of new spawned life
Anonymous to history, blind to their purpose.

Above them, bellowing sea lions,
Prowling mastodons once scavenged
Fish abundant enough to fill every belly that has ever
Hungered.

Why have they gone?

Here now, in scattering foam a found conch, its glistening chambers
Echo an infinite catalogue of lost and unnamed images.
Will our races become modern memoriam?

Or, as I perceive within these fragile catacombs,
A promised assurance of another Plan.
Free to choose eternal life,
Saved from another, a mortal
Extinction?

Song Of Faith —

Faith is the essence of life.
Without it we cannot live, we cannot prosper.
Love cannot grow, harvest is never seen.

Faith is a miracle of existence.
The essential plum of life, eternal and of long standing.
It cannot be extinguished. Our guiding light from Heaven,
What the universe is to God.

Faith is eternal in all His creations.
All things are in supplication to Him.
His word is perfect and long standing.
His voice is all pervading and all comforting.
Nothing can exist without God.
He is the marvel of creation.

Darkness, pain and suffering
Define a faithless life, blind to fruitful destiny
In any course, at any price. A childish understanding, stopped up,
Futile and of small worth.

Be faithful in all things.
What is required for good will be thine.
God will supply thee with thy needs.
Take thy faith with thee as a purse goeth.
Find there those jewels which God has put for those who love Him.

Our Father's love is founder to faith,
Sharing its eternity. Greater still than our own care
One for another. His eternal flame is always lit
For us. We are the product of His love.

Be of good cheer, then!
When the Savior comes to call, to reign upon this earth
To rule in love and mercy, we'll feel the extent of his love
And through him we will find and fulfill ourselves.

Estimated Time of Arrival —

At noon
Over Point Conception
The sun cuts a hat of light from the shadows
And caps the skull of the earth
Cutting the night into silhouette
From Canberra to Aleutia to the Arctic.
It slips and spills down across America
Into the cool Atlantic
Where it drowns . . . .

The sun ignores the Eskimo men of Resolute
Dreaming near their spears,
Eating only memories of fat brown seals
Not yet arrived — their images still blowing
Through the ice, moles of the seas
Cracking through the nights
Like rollicking thieves.

The women sit,
Wrapped in patience, furred amulets
Facing the long, shadowed wilderness
Where nothing is certain beyond thickets
Of grass, or heather growing
On green-gray stone.
Or famine reawakening like a monster
At their backs.

They sit and carve images of white bears
Watching their reflections unchanging on black stone.
But now the Borealis rises with life
Through the vastness, twisting with color
Like a cracking whip!

It is a sign.
The seals return, children shout.
Women rise to ready the sleds

And the men will hunt.

They shall chant now, pray their thanks,
Their fate is in the Hand
That turns the earth from darkness' veil
Toward the Perfect Light.

Song of the Christ —

We are the children of our Christ
Lord of Kings, only Begotten Son of God
Molded by thy master hand
Deemed worthy of this hallowed land [1]
Followers of the gospel's iron rod.

To the course that rounds our lives
O Savior bring thy timeless love
To we who live at thy behest [2]
Thou ministers and proves our best.
Thou knows our lives, our faith, our home above.

Thou wast sent by He who formed thee
In the belly of a maid
She birthed thee in that humble room
So unlike the heav'nly womb [3]
Where death and sin dwell not, nor price be paid.

Thou came and died amongst our kind
But from that tomb, thy cave of stone
Thou rose and took thy life again [4]
Then walked among the sons of men.
That we might live new seeds of life were sown [5]

O, Sower of eternal lives
Let us prepare a path for thee
Of spirits who will serve their Christ [6]
A bridge of love and sacrifice
Meet for thy innocence and purity.

Give us this day thy bread of life
The sacrament of broken crust
That it may lead us to our Feast
Of endless life [7], that e'en the least
Can know his King who reigns among the just.

O help me now, my precious Lord
To see again thy radiant face
To bask forever in thy light
Thy shield that crushed the heel of night [8]
Before the awesome bounty of thy perfect grace.

---

[1] *Ether 2:10, Mos 29:32*

[2] *Mormon 9:17*

[3] *Gen 1:27*

[4] *Matt 28:7,9-20, 3Ne 9:21-22*

[5] *Alma 11:40-45*

[6] *Mormon 9:27-29*

[7] *3Ne 15:9; 2Ne 9:13*

[8] *D&C 136:32-33*

VOICES BEYOND THE VEIL —

Yea, behold, I will tell you in your mind and in your heart, by the Holy Ghost, which shall come upon you and which shall dwell in your heart. Now, behold, this is the spirit of revelation . . .

— Doctrine and Covenants 8:2,3.

Behold, the Lord has shown unto me great and marvelous things . . .

— Mormon 8:34.

The gift of revelation is limited only by man's capacity to receive it.

I am William the repentant —

This is my testimony of repentance. Repentance is the only way Heavenly Father will accept us in His legion. When I was young I committed all manner of sinfulness. I was promiscuous and I indulged in many other pastimes that were not correct in God's eyes. Oh, my crimes were not great ones, but crimes against myself, and they needed to be totally forgiven. I was not then aware of the saving power of Christ, our master.

When I finally was awakened to my Father in Heaven's plan for my life I came to Him in sincere repentance and asked mightily for the forgiveness I knew I needed before proceeding further. He laid out a Plan for me that led directly to Him. I followed that path and repentance paved the way for me to arrive there. I had to participate in the process fully before the Lord would forgive and forget the liaison between myself and my sinfulness. I fell upon my face many times and asked with an increasingly humble heart for God's awareness of all my sins and his focusing upon them because I needed the help of my Father to become whole once more.

I was cleansed of all sin and because I was cleansed I am a new man and I feel wonderful. In the mortal world we are tested and tried by the Adversary. We need all our strength to resist him. I surely am not worthy of the highest glory, I feel, but without repentance I would be worth far less. I could not abide that darkness and distance from the Lord Jesus Christ who comes to visit me in my afflictions and who will comfort me for eternity.

I love the Lord my God, I sing his praises all day and night. He is wondrous to behold. He shines and radiates love from all corners of creation. He has come to smile upon me. I fall at his feet. I am all amazed at the love Jesus has for me, his errant son who was blind, but now I see. Glory be to the Highest and to the Son of God, who comes to me.

I would tell you to bide your time well in the human abode and learn the ways of the Kingdom in your heart, your home and your daily lives. Come unto Christ with a true and repentant heart that longs to free itself of earthly cares, free of the shackles of sin. Rise above it all to the heavens that await you. Give up your trespasses and you will know your Savior, elude the Adversary and his legions. Cleansed, you will come forth in the First Resurrection. Grow and progress toward your eternal salvation that awaits you here in the eternities.

I am Miriam, the fisherwoman —

I have a knowledge of Jesus Christ in a very direct way, as I have seen him in life and again in death. I was among the women who saw him in Jerusalem. I was on the Mount of Olives when he spoke to us. We were gathered together, having heard his wondrous voice before. It was sonorous, of great power and calm, hard to hear yet clear until it sounded inside oneself. He came to us in a whisper, softly, without fanfare and without time, it seemed. And he stayed long enough to answer all our questions, and we had many. We stayed with him and asked him many things.

I was given the privilege of seeing the Savior in person, before his death on the cross. He was fair of face, handsome in a stern but not a self possessed way. He spoke with great authority and we all listened to him. He was profound, he spoke of the resurrection of the soul and spirit. He told us of his Father in Heaven and of the heaven that awaits us all. He was not curt but exacting, taking us to him one by one and blessing us on the head and shoulders. His smile, I remember, was beautific and his mien was of innocence, simple and yet beautiful, so that we knew he was the Christ.

Each of us bowed to him, eventually, before he left us. He proclaimed the kingdom of heaven was at hand and that he had come to save us all through his death on the cross that had been put there for the redemption of all nations in the coming years.

I remember that we all loved and respected him. He spoke with brilliance and, taking someone beneath his wing he taught them as one having total authority. He commanded the wind be still that we might listen and hear him without disturbance. He was and is a perfect man. All that he proclaimed is coming to pass upon the earth and for me now in the spirit.

I love my Jesus the Christ. I have learned many things here at his knee and I am forever grateful to him.

I am Florence, the convert —

When I was very young I committed sins. I was always sharp to my mother and I did not honor her or my father much. I was willful and often had my say in life. But when I grew up I found the Church through learning about the Prophet Joseph Smith and I fully repented of my behavior. I believed his story and I knew God had spoken through him. I loved him. The work has been done for me in a temple of the Lord.

The principle of repentance is eternal. We only know what we find on earth and what our leaders tell us, but here in the eternities, waiting for our Savior to again descend to earth, we know that repentance is a perfect principle of salvation. It cures the world of its ills. Salvation is freedom from sin and repentance. Where the soul has become perfect no repenting is necessary, but that takes millennia. On earth we need to repent all the time and to be faithful in all we do that we can come before the Father at the end of life and have His blessing and the blessings of the brethren here and in the church here in Heaven. I see the prophets here teaching thousands upon thousands the truth and those souls are having to go through deep repentance for the mess they made of their lives on earth.

If we don't repent we ask the Lord to accept us as we are now on earth. He will do so, but he places us where we can get greater understanding and help for our troubles and illnesses of our spirit. To not repent is to not cleanse the spirit and not want to be with God after this life is over. The devil has his tricks and he will come to you and offer you rewards that are not of God in order that you will follow him. Bring repentance into your life and watch sin leave it.

Without repentance being available we are always in the dark and cannot learn to love properly, because we cannot see the good in God or in ourselves. We have been given the mind and will of God and we are capable on earth of all that He is or has or can do, through the Priesthood. When we do not take advantage of our ability to repent we forfeit that wondrous ability to know our own worth and that of our Father, for that pathway is never opened and set before us. The feast of life demands that we cleanse ourselves of all unrighteousness and strive to be faithful to the Lord and his teachings.

I testify to you that repentance is a true principle.

I am Margo, the inspired one —

My life was hard. I was the daughter of a farmer in Iowa and we raised pigs, hogs, chicken, beef. I worked hard there until I met my husband to be. We moved away and raised our children. In my difficult childhood I found much peace in the love of the Lord who inspired me to work hard and to love my parents and my husband.

Marshall was so good and sweet to me we got along right away. I would come to him and tell him of my great love of Christ. He knew how I felt and he returned that love. We went on to live lives that were uplifted by the knowledge that our Savior is always with us and that he feeds us his truths as we eat, sleep and walk, as we pray and as we contemplate our lives. I am always inspired of God to write and play and sing and to tell of the beauty of Heaven and the beauty and perfection of our Lord.

Inspiration is a word used to denote a feeling of oneness with God, a feeling of peace in His presence and of insight into His basic wants for us and His need of us in His life. When I was on the earth I came into contact with an inspired minister who taught me the order of prayer at an early age. I prayed mightily to the Father in hopes he would hear me. I asked to be inspired of Him that I might know the testimony of truth. He responded with the most beautiful and perfect prayer in return. I felt inspired to write it down and have always kept it. I sing now to tell the world the truth of the beauty of Heaven and the beauty and perfection of our Lord in Heaven.

Inspiration brings me peace. When I think on the beautiful surroundings He has prepared for us I am amazed and beautified in His presence. I feel beauty is within me and I radiate it outward to others I meet. I am always in His presence and the presence of my Lord, because they care for me and sends angels after me to do their work within me. Sing the praises of the Lord. He is perfect in his robes of white and red and he comes often to all those who love him. Now in Heaven we see him often and we love and adore him forevermore. He comes soon to the generations of mankind to adjudicate them

I am Marvin, the accountant —

I was a retired accountant, a banker. My early life was of the sort that knew much trouble. I went to bed at night sometimes very unhappy and afraid of tomorrow and what it would bring. When I was a boy I heard of a man who said he knew what the truths of the world were and I went to see him. He was big and strong and handsome. He told me I lacked a certain faith in the Savior who is Jesus Christ. He gave me a book and sent me home to read it and I did read it. I came away convinced that Jesus is the Christ and that I had to follow him to find any happiness anywhere. I have learned to love others and to serve them in charity.

When I was grown I was involved in many affairs of state and knew many famous people. Never in my adult life have I known of anyone who matched my love of Christ or my fervor for the gospel as it was written there in that book. I live my entire life with inspiration for my Savior and his kingdom there in Heaven. I have dreamed that he is perfect beyond description and demure and lovely and loving to all who he meets. I believe he is coming to earth again soon to finish the world's work and to bind Satan, but no one knows where he will be received there.

I had six children with my beautiful wife and we taught them all to love Christ and to long for his kingdom. My life is only inspired because of my lifelong devotion to those few but true principles. I learned right away that insolence before God is an abomination. I prided myself on righteous living and attained a wealthy and happy status because of it.

What inspired me is the knowledge that Jesus our Savior loves us all and that he helps us to do what is right that we can be blessed. Inspiration is of God and the Holy Ghost who comes and tells us what we need to know to re-enter the kingdom of Heaven. If we ascribe to that instruction we will be exalted above and we will see our Heavenly Father again. I always tried to live in such a way that I could count on seeing my family again and we are all here now, awaiting the return of our Savior to the earth, that our family may live together eternally.

I am Randall, the believer —

This is a testimony of faith in Heavenly Father. When I was young a man came to me and said I needed more faith in God. I pretended to believe him to see what he was up to. He presented me with a book and urged me to read it. I did so and was caught up in it. I knew it to be true and decided to live my life in accordance with this book. I have since found that faith is the measure of belief we all have in what we read, see, imagine and divine to be true. I know the precepts put forth in this book, called the Book of Mormon, are true and I have embraced it all my life with the same fervor I have for life.

I have found over the years when my faith in humanity was lessened the lessons in this book helped me to promote my personal understanding until I could no longer endure being without complete faith in God and His wondrous power to convert minds and hearts to His will. When we agree that God's will is greatest among all, our faith is immeasurably strengthened. There are many precepts in the Book of Mormon worth hearkening to. The principles therein are full of light of truth, and one who follows in the path of Christ is bound to grow to love him and to have enormous faith in the truth he presented from his Father in Heaven. I personally gained a great testimony just listening, reading and praying to know the true way.

I am new here in the spirit world, learning constantly and gaining even greater assurance that the principles presented in the Bible and the Book of Mormon are true.

I am Martin, the hero —

I was a wartime hero. When I was in the Vietnam war a shrapnel bomb exploded beneath my feet. I immediately felt weak and in shock and fainted away. When I came to, I was on a stretcher in the jungle and my back and face were both torn. I screamed in agony many times throughout the long, torturous nights that followed until an Army sergeant came to call on me and read to me from the Bible. He talked about Jesus Christ and how he had accepted onto himself all of our pain and how we owed him our lives. If we had to die for what we believe in we would be like him.

His words made my pain easier and I immediately felt better. When I was released to go home I knew that faith had brought me through it all. There was a time in my life when faith was just a word, and a bad one at that, because I didn't believe. But now I know that we all need to be faithful and diligent when we are working for the Lord, and that is all the time. My faith helped to pull me through the war, to bind up my psychic wounds and to become an effective person again.

I am Charles, the architect —

I come here today to tell thee about my love of my Savior, who is Jesus Christ. When I was a boy I lived in England and Wales in 1880. Jesus came to me and gave me the spirit of discernment and service through prophecy in that I could "see" the results of the right and wrong in my life and the lives of others whose lives were marred by unhappy occurrences. By means of receiving premonitions of danger to others I could help them avoid problems or to at least work through them. I was an architect and built many beautiful structures. None of my buildings were churches but I built a monastery for all the monks there. I found solace in doing the works of Christ and became a staunch follower of his. I followed the Savior throughout my life there on earth and I died I came here to spirit prison where he comes and ministers.

Christ is my Savior. I see him here and I speak with him. When I was on earth he came to me often and told me of his love for me and his devotion to all mankind. All in my family were followers and went to church when we could. I was a Catholic then and I loved my church. I remember going before the altar and praying to better know my Savior, to get his blessings upon my head and for my life.

I believe in Christ. In all the marvelous ways he changed my heart from a boy to that of a man, bent upon service and love of others. I became a god fearing man. My family was not devout but I developed a real love for the gospel as it was taught to me and I loved to recite the missal and to say the prayers out loud in Latin and in English. My wife in later years was a practicing Catholic as well, and we were both happy to attend the church of the Lord.

Christ gave me the foresight to look beyond myself and to see all that is there. He gave me great insight and purpose. He came to me at a time when I was low and feeling unloved and without purpose and gave me power to make my own life worthy. He gave me the ability to see that life without love is purposeless and that I could never achieve what I wanted in life without his help. He gave me greater love for the Father and for the Son, which he is. He gave me all that I possess and ever will possess. He is my father and I love him mightily. That is my testimony.

My name is Alan, the merchant —

I am a Christian from France. I lived in Vichy in my youth and became a very successful merchant, always giving fealty to my Father in Heaven and my Christ. I became enamored of a woman there and Jesus helped me to see that she was not the proper one for me. I later married into a large family where I was given exclusive reign of the place. I married well and we had several children, all of whom are righteous beings and who have gone far in life. I feel that Jesus has come to me, waiting upon me that I might understand him and his purpose among us. He is sweet and gentle with us all.

I am a happy man today because of what I know of Christ. He has come to tell us all that the world is his and God's and that they want us to inherit it from them and live side by side with them in harmony and peacefulness. I have had revelations from them. They abhor war and dissension. My Savior has helped me to sort out my problems with my children so they would worship our Heavenly Father. When first I had revelation of him I hearkened right away. He is magnetic, he pulls people to him through his inner strength and beauty and innocence.

The Lord has prompted me to start a successful business and to marry well. He has changed my heart so it is not cold but warm and friendly. He has watched me grow and urged me on to greater things. He is my Redeemer and he has given me the hope that I may once again see my God in Heaven. Jesus Christ is the perfect one and I worship him as well as the Father in Heaven.

I know that Jesus the Christ is the Savior of the world, that he came to us to help us and to lead us back to him that the Father may have his children back again with Him. I know that Jesus has far to go to see all of us who love him and who are faithful to him and that he has much to do each day of our lives to edify our existence upon the earth. I know that he is with us in the eternities. On earth he will soon reign for one thousand years in righteousness. I know that I love and cherish him and his presence with me. I am his disciple and I love his long suffering for all of us because we can now learn how to survive together forever.

I am Fred, the faithful —

I was a special person on earth. As an accountant I handled large sums of money for a brokerage firm and I was particularly blessed with faith during my life. It wasn't always easy to find it when I needed it, but happily I always found it. Faith in the Lord is uppermost in my mind now, but when I was growing up there were many life issues which required faith like that of my ancestors, but I couldn't find the energy to make that desire real.

I was working one night when I felt faint. I had diabetes and took regular insulin shots. I had fallen into some kind of coma-like state. When I awoke I was alone, everyone else had left the building. I could not get out and had to spend the night there alone. It was an awful experience. I remember praying throughout the night and when morning came there were no faces nearby to speak with. I learned faith that night, to depend solely on the Lord for my sustenance and to bring myself down to a humble level so he could administer to me.

I have many stories which engender faith in life. Let me tell you one, of that dark afternoon of fear and longing for those things that are never fulfilled. It was a rainy night on the railroad. I was then an agent on duty in the building and in sole charge. A man came into the shop. He wore a funny jacket on and a sour look. He held me up for the money in the safe, small amount though it was. I immediately called my superiors and they came to see if they could help. The man had left the building, he was headed to town in a white truck. We followed after him until we reached him and arrested him for trespassing and theft. He went to jail. It was my faith that saved me because I did not give in to him. I gave him the money but I retained my courage and my self-possession.

My faith had seen me through it all and forever it helps me in all that I have done.

We are Marv and Gina,
the charitable —

I am Marv. When I was young I lived in a southern state. We were poor and had little to farm and to eat. Once I happened upon a rabbit trapped in a trap by a hunter. I freed him but his leg was broken, poor thing. I took him home and splinted the leg and it healed in a matter of weeks. When my family realized that I had a rabbit and it was meat, they wanted to kill and eat it. I wouldn't let them do so. I took the rabbit out and let it go, knowing that freedom to that rabbit was more important to God than meat for my family. Charity is the pure love that one exhibits to another and it flows as living water throughout our souls.

A little while later a cow was brought to us for milking and that cow came to be known as Dinner. We raised it and eventually slaughtered it and gave it to all of our family to eat. We were extremely grateful to that cow for its donation of its body to us for meat and milk.

꽃

I am Gina and I will share a story with you. I've had many experiences with charitable living. Once, when I was small my mother took me to a doctor for my swollen foot. She was very beautiful. We went to the doctor and he fixed my foot. He told us he would not charge us as he knew my mother had little to pay him with. Nevertheless, he looked after us as a father for many years, checking our bodies and giving us many free services. I know this was because we were poor and had not enough even to cover ourselves. Charitable works have surrounded my all my life and I have tried mightily to repay the blessing with my own measure of giving freely.

I am he who walked among you —

I will give thee a story of charity. When I preached along the Sea of Galilee a great storm grew up. When I walked on the water to Peter he turned to me and said "Master, I come to thee," but he soon lost faith and fell into the water. I gave out my hand to him and he took it and was saved, but how many of us take the hand of another who can save us from death? I am the living water, the way and the way back from death.

My own death and resurrection was the greatest charity of all and few there be who find the way to me and to my kingdom, which is the kingdom of the Father as well. The great charity of the Father is that He has made possible for us the way to come home through the hearts of others and through our own solemn testimony of the truth of His kingdom.

Charity works in a way different from all other things, it must be given without remuneration and with no hope of reward. Too many are eager for reward and do not love with a full heart. Be kind to all whom you meet and love them with a full heart, knowing you are sisters and brothers, and that is charity enough, for a large part.

We take it for granted but the world perishes in disbelief and in coldness to others. We need to be aware of others and be giving toward them that they will be giving to all who come within their range of view. They must ask themselves what is charitable about each person that is memorable and that can be presented to me and to my Father.

We are waiting for them to repent and come unto me and to my Father. That is the most important thing they can know at this time.

STORYTIME

Boundaries —

That, they should seek the Lord . . . feel after him, and find him, though he be not far from every one of us — The Acts 17:27

1 Texas! Country that once suffered a portion of the wandering nation of Israel, far from their home in Jerusalem. After centuries of disastrous infighting these transplanted Hebrews — who were once led by prophets — had divided into hundreds of dangerous tribes, including the murderous Comanche and Apache, who called the south-western states their home.

Not long after the Lone Star State's lusty, bloody history was tamed by the ink of treaties, seekers of a spiritual bounty trod in peace as harvesters of souls. Sister DiNate and I, Sister Davis, were among her most recent explorers as newly set apart, full time proselytizing missionaries for The Church of Jesus Christ of Latter-day Saints. Sitting high like royalty in her old 4-wheel drive Jeep, Bambina, we were here to claim Texas for the Lord. It was summer and hot breezes swirled. We were checking out our new area, looking for tracting possibilities second to a place to eat and all the while shaking our heads in wonder as I read from the moldy history book in my lap.

"When the French traders and Catholic missionaries hit Canada, it wasn't long before their presence was felt throughout the interior of the country. But they could not tame such a light-filled land. The region of the Appalachians now lay open to conquest, now the whole continent was open to exploration. So vast and promising were her fertile plains and plentiful rivers that she bore the onslaught of six more foreign nations willing to bargain death for her charms. Finally, promises of peace lured her settlers away from war and into a greater, divinely wrought Union, but those who love her know that within her verdant boundaries many treasures still await gathering."

Maria Faustina Barretti DiNate, her ample Italian body moving with the jolts of the hilly roads, clucked in understanding while I droned on. Her large black eyes hid behind a cascade of charcoal lashes. She was un-impressed. Her family had long ago left the rich Calabrian coastal region of southern Italy for the chilly cloistered shores of New England, hoping for American prosperity and Yankee good luck. Several generations later when her family had spread across the wintry slopes of Vermont they occasionally welcomed missionaries in from the snow. These faithful youth shared a new and urgent message with the Catholic emigrants. Maria Faustina Barretti was one of few who knew they spoke the truth. She followed them to baptism. A year later she married her childhood companion, Joseph, who worked in the marble quarries of Barre, and they began their own family. Maria had just celebrated with Joseph his fifty-fourth birthday when the accident in the quarry took the lives of nine men of the town, Joseph's among them. Maria was devastated. She clung to her children for a time until the Lord stirred her heart to his own purpose. With many deep sighs and customary attention to duty, Maria prayed about it with her bishop and her children on a Sunday. The next day she filled out papers for a mission. When she was called to Texas, she said

"This can't be true. I don't know no one there."

Then she packed her bags and drove across the country to Provo, Utah and the Senior Missionary Training Center.

Across the continent from Maria DiNate I had also worn "widow weeds". My own history was hard to trace past my Bohemian grandparents. I was born in woody central Oregon, a northern terminus of the Mormon Trail, where there may be as many words to describe rain as the Eskimos have for snow. The Northwest is a place conducive eight months of any year to indoor study and contemplation, so early on I embraced a life of research. I'd just decided I'd never marry when I found Michael, a brick mason and construction worker. We were almost thirty. We married in the shadow of Mt. Rainier and dreamed of many children, but none answered our call. In our loneliness for family we opened our home to many of God's little wayfarers and it brought us a closeness that was wondrous and surprising. During those years we joined the Church and were sealed for time and eternity. But then the Lord let my husband know that his time here would be cut short. Our last year together was spent in hospitals.

When Michael passed on, my own life was diminished. I returned to work, but it could not fill me. That is when the Lord beckoned. I felt the unmistakable call to serve and happily responded. When I learned my mission destination was Texas I thought of longhorn steer and huge fruit. Now that I was here being jostled around in an old Jeep with my new companion, I realized how small my world had been.

I think we were both amazed to find ourselves far from comfort zones and familiar people. And we were scared, I'll admit it, having just arrived at our mission area the day before, so we talked to keep ourselves brave and tried to appear mellow. Neither of us had ever been to any part of Texas, so our new bishop loaned us a book of state history. I read while we drove, trying to comprehend the endless green pastures and lush woods of south central Texas.

"Remember the word 'south', a native of Texas had cautioned me before we left Senior MTC. "Central Texas is definitely part of the new South."

In the humid summer stillness we breathed in the dust that still clung to the air. Bluebells waved at us from their grassy loams. Shrubs of honey mesquite with crooked branches beckoned us. I looked up just in time to see a red cardinal flutter by. There was a kind of lowing music in the air, pushed around by the sultry wind.

"This place has quite a past. Spain laid claim to Florida and Texas, held on with a death grip, even when John Quincy Adams demanded it back. Then Mexico got hold of it . . . they still think they made a mistake in offering land to Americans for nothing. We finally fought a bloody war with them over this place. Wow! Texas. Maybe we're traveling over some of those historic battlegrounds right now, do you suppose?"

Traveling always did that to me, got me excited in the history of a place, what it must have been like when our country's mantle was newly upon it, the mysteries and changes we could only read about. I looked out at the miles of whitewashed fence that lined the old two-lane highway like a stiff lace border, or like a crown. Couch grass grew around the wood. Suddenly it became markers along an endless line of fire. Victory on one side, defeat on the other.

"We are as the armies of Helaman," my mind sang. "We are marching onto glory; We are working for our crown." Soldiers to the front, battle stations! We are part of the female contingent of the Lord's senior regiment, tried and true patriots in the spiritual army of God. Well, why not? Right here in the languid peacefulness of south central Texas, beyond the barns and cattle, there were souls searching for the truth. They were meant for us to find and rescue. What was our battle cry? Baptize, baptize!

The voice of my new companion broke my reverie.

"This Texas is nothing like in Vermont,"

Sister DiNate observed this while negotiating a turn past some horse-back riders plodding across the highway in front of us.

"In Vermont you have water everywhere, Lake Champlain, full of boats. Ice skating, yes! Four hundred lakes. Now that's territory! I got lots of family in Barre, that's French, bar-aay. Cousins, nieces and lots of nephews, yes. I bet you this truck they all sitting down to a nice fettuccine right now." She sighed heavily, savoring memorable meals from her very recent past.

"Pasta would be nice," I said. "My late husband and I ate a lot of kasha. It's a western European treat. In this country they call it buckwheat groats. You can buy it in health food stores, lots of those in Oregon. It's great, cooks up into a kind of rice. Goes naturally with meatballs or a nice roast and potatoes. Gosh, I'm getting hungry again. What are we doing for dinner?"

Sister DiNate sighed. Her heavy gray mane was falling out of its ornate barrette. She said her hair had been a rich ebony that in her teens cascaded "luxuriously" down her back.

"Ah, who can say? Second day in south central Texas. What is a Tex-as? No Italians, no prospects, no family, no restaurants. It's no Vermont. But my Joseph, he know what to do. Always he finds a good restaurant, he knew to order. I miss my Joseph, mama mia." She heaved another sigh and spurred Bambina forward.

I commiserated. My Michael was a sweet man, a beautiful guy, big and wide. He worked the big jobs. Always out in the weather. I think that's what finally took him, the lousy northwest weather. We loved to travel whenever we could get away. Why, he took me to seven states in a month one year! Washington to the Dakotas and on down and around, in a kind of backward "C". We saw all the monuments, even went through the Grand Canyon. Sometimes we'd have a contest to see who could name all the cities of the Union, and he finally won. But I could name all the temples. It had been three years since the Lord called him home again, but my memories were vivid as the pictures in the history book.

We were coming to a small grocery, the only store since leaving the main highway over an hour ago. It was dilapidated and empty of custom-ers. Broken bits of beer bottles were scattered around the lot. A cat sat on a post nearby, watching hungrily the crows that pecked for crumbs in the dirt. It didn't look inviting.

"Let's pass it by, maybe there's something down the road, a restaurant, you know? We can eat a real dinner, maybe." Sister DiNate drove on. "This isn't Vermont," she said. "They may not even serve pasta in Texas." She turned suddenly and her coal eyes stared at mine, as if the thought was incredulous to her. "What will I do if I have to wait a whole year to eat pasta?" Her hands gripped the wheel at the thought.

I tried not to laugh.

"We'll get by, somehow. Remember the pioneering spirit! We're here to convert souls to the Gospel of Jesus Christ. Pasta and kasha may have to wait. The world as we know it is on hold. This —" I waved my arm across the vista of grass before us — "is a new world." But she was shaking her head sadly. "Si`, e`vero, e` vero. It's true."

Our new assignment was to a territory known the world over for its wide plains and thick stands of pine and box elder forests. Some of the country's finest cattle stock was bred in Texas, as well as — if you'd believe it — the "biggest and bestest" of everything. Even the weather obliged by being 80's when both our home states were on Storm Alert. But to Sister DiNate, Texas was a foreign country, even compared to Vermont. She missed things Italianate and familiar.

True, we might have to settle for black-eyed peas and corn bread for a year. My own memory kept returning to the valley below St. Helens. I reminisced of the mountains and the Straits, camping and fishing for vanishing salmon with Michael in freezing northern lakes. I shared her sense of displacement, but what could we do? We were volunteers, badge-wearing missionaries fresh from training, stoked with faith and hope and intent upon doing our part to save worthy souls, though only the few would discern our true identity as messengers of the Lord. It was a romantic view of life, but one that persisted.

If you look at a globe of our world and imagine for a moment only those who have come forth to be missionaries of The Church of Jesus Christ of Latter-day Saints walking bravely amid the people of the earth, and then expand that number to include the multitudes who have sprung from those courageous pioneers and from the loins of those who they converted, why, it would be staggering! That in itself is a marvelous work and wonder. Sacrifice? With pleasure, sir. Time? That's what time is for. Joy? Just a baptism away. It would all come together. Just as soon as we two aging but dedicated (more than a little scared), citified and somewhat befuddled sisters could make it happen.

And south central Texas would be our proving ground. The world for us centered upon a stretch of warm fenced pasture spanning thirty miles in every direction. In his office, our Mission President Fowler showed us on his map of America "the great state of Texas." Across the top and sides of the map were taped 2" square head shots of elders and sisters who were currently serving within in the Texas mission boundaries. I was surprised to find DiNate's and my own picture already in place beside the beaming young Elders assigned to our branch. He pointed to a red circled area a good measure south of the Dallas-Fort Worth metroplex.

"You'll be in the plains and in rolling hill country. For the next twelve months the worlds of Oregon and Vermont will not exist. You'll live, breathe and work within your new boundaries. You'll need to visit all the people in your area. Find them and teach them, bring them in. You're not going to a stake or a ward, my sweet sisters, but to a branch. A branch that must become a stake, a rod in the hand of the Lord in time. Your being there must help to make that miracle happen. Plan on very few transfers, we have lots of members who are very lax about attending their meetings within your branch boundaries, and you will be responsible for bringing in those sheep. Do you have the picture? The Lord will bless you for your service."

We tried to get the picture. We prayed for a new mindset, diligently imagining ourselves as stoic shepherds in the wilderness of American Texas, but the vision was comical. Instead of hardy outdoor men we were aging women used to soft indoor lives. We had skirts around our calves instead of woolen pants and capes. In place of water flasks, cheese and bread we toted purses and were never without our signature 6 x 10 inch scripture cases. Of course, the Book of Mormon was our staff. But whereas leaders of woolly flocks typically grow up alongside their charges, we had just been rewarded with a vast chunk of acreage which consisted mainly of forlorn barns, horses, cows and endless fields of dandelions, sunflowers and sticky poppies. Worst of all, we had no figurative sheep. Some shepherds!

The week before, Sister DiNate and I had met at MTC. We were introduced at the first meeting. Immediately I liked her. I felt an imperative to be with her. She took me in her strong arms and pressed a warm cheek to mine.

"Ben`e, mi amica, ben`e, e` vero," she said, and then we both cried a little. A week later we threw our bags into her old Jeep and headed south to find our new home. Now we shared the duties, she drove, chose the restaurants and kept Bambina happy while I kept track of the mileage, meal tickets and read history. It was a long and thoughtful ride and we used it to get acquainted.

With the southeast tilt came new greenery, the piney woods, berry bushes, armadillos and scrumptious smells of southern baking. I favored the spirit of progress with The Yellow Rose of Texas while my new companion sang exclusively Italian to keep herself (and me) awake. I think I heard Volare forty times by actual count.

Late on the second night we arrived at our destination, spurred on by the theme from The Barber of Seville. Very much in need of sleep, we walked together into our new home. That is when it really hit us that we were on a mission. The door opened upon a venerable second story apartment that had been for years a make-do refuge for arriving and transferring sister missionaries. Everything our eyes took in was old and silent. The rooms were starkly unwelcoming. What furniture we found was scarred up, broken, third hand old and just plain ugly. Curtains and drapes were missing from the windows. The walls were cold. The place was empty of the things that make a house a home. We stood there, not really comprehending it all, two tired widows trying to be brave.

The living room was most impersonal. It reminded me of a motel I'd stayed in with Michael in years past when he was ill. A plaid couch still sagged from the many weights placed upon it. A large lamp with a horrible bulbous orange base lurked on the floor near the couch. A tan colored "coffee table" that was covered with crayon scrawls was covered with pamphlets the former sister missionaries had left for us.

It was grim. But a sweet spirit permeated the air, nevertheless. We have a history, too, the room seemed to say. Marvelous things have happened here. Now we are waiting to be filled with your spirit. A picture of Jesus Christ hung on the wall near the door, as if to comfort us —

Don't worry, it said, these things are only temporal. I am the light and the life in this place and I am with thee always. It was our only warm thought.

The picture window in the front looked out on the back of a red and white brick carriage-type house with a screened-in front porch, the style I have read is always found in southern states. I thought it charming. Sister

DiNate took one long look and sighed heavily.

"Ah," she said softly. "That's the place we need."

We tried not to be too disappointed. True, it was not like my cozy, modern home in Oregon, with lush, soft furniture, full of light and color. I would miss my hundreds of books, the pictures of Michael and I near the TV and on the night stand next to our bed, but it would have to do. I looked over at Sister DiNate. I knew her home was large and very often crowded. She'd told me her relatives filled it with visits and lots of rich food, with laughter and passion for life. Home to her was a large and well-stocked kitchen, a dining room set off by Italianate rococo wallpaper that always smelled faintly of roasted garlic and fennel. This was going to be a serious adjustment for each of us.

"What do you think, Sister? It's not Vermont?"

Sister DiNate's hands spread into the air before her in that Italian gesture that defies explanation. She raised her chin defiantly.

"Oh, what can I say, it's . . . small. No room for cooking. "This —" she walked around a counter to the utilitarian stove and single sink and slapped it — "is not a kitchen. Where would my family sit? Smell. If a place is to be a home, it must to smell. Oregano, garlic, tomatoes. Ahh."

She said "tomahtos" and her voice rose in anticipation. But in her lovely eyes there was the start of tears.

The bathroom did have a good shower, except for the black curtain. It had a small window that allowed us to take in the top of a huge magnolia tree that shaded the town's only park, a good place for meeting with referrals and prospects. The bedroom was another story. Its twin beds, a small night stand and a very old mahogany dresser had been generously donated years ago by the late Junipero Leandro of the Sierra Ranch, north of us. His family owned this and many other old apartment buildings. The mattresses were worn soft. A dresser drawer was missing its bottom slat. The thermostat on the wall was broken and there was no toilet paper in the bathroom. There was no bedding, no lamp, no plants nor pictures. It was a room devoted to sleeping, a task as basic as the washing of hair. Sister DiNate and I sat on our beds and stared at the cold walls, feeling the task ahead of us already too heavy, and then we sighed and stared at one another. Finally, we went out to find the local department store before meeting the branch president and his family for dinner.

2 If we were worried about feeling comfortable and upholstered in our appointed quarters, many of those concerns were mended with the needle of time. We were expected. Branch members were notified we had arrived. They baked and they cooked. They called on members who hadn't been to church in months and they cooked and baked. The bishop's wife invited us to take ivy cuttings and provided pots. Brother Werner came dutifully to the door in overalls with his ladder and toolbox. Brother Gonzales and his wife and four little girls gave us blankets and pillows. Sister Jenny Thomas found some throw rugs that matched the bedroom carpet. Her neighbor had sharpened slicing and paring knives and glass baking dishes she had been keeping in storage to give to her nieces. She gave them to us instead. The apartment manager fixed the thermostat and apologized for the coldness of the place.

"I'll see what I can do about replacing that awful lamp," he said, scratching his bald head. "Maybe the couch can be replaced, too. What color do you want?"

Mormon hospitality or southern, it was wonderful. I discovered an herbal store and bought a supply of the cleansing herb, echinacea. Sister DiNate, when she found that the local market carried elephant garlic, bought a bagful and right there in front of the bin sang a few happy phrases from the opera Don Giovanni. We got two referrals that afternoon.

That night we made a list of all those in the branch and used that as our initial prayer list, adding to it many who we met during the entire year, until every morning upon rising it took us a long time to prayerfully ask Heavenly Father for his generous blessings in their behalf.

Nine a.m. was Fast and Testimony meeting in a typical LDS building. We pressed our Sunday dresses on new ironing boards, congratulated each other on making it through the first week and bravely went forth to get better acquainted. The building was small, with a tiny playroom next to the smaller library that boasted only a wall of books alongside the office partition. Elders Jackson and Brown of Bountiful and Logan respectively, greeted us warmly. Branch President Howard was thrilled to see us. A towering man, he had the presence of someone who couldn't wait to get things done. His branch had been six months without sister missionaries. He and the members had prayed mightily to be blessed with new recruits and they were all smiles when we arrived.

We were brought up to date on meetings and locations, zone leaders and so on, then introduced around. Brother Werner was there with his German wife, Helga. They'd arrived recently from east Texas to start a repair business. Brother Werner had seen much "evil goings on" in his native Germany during the 30's. He planned an escape to America. Shortly after arriving at Ellis Island he heard someone speak derogatorily of the Church, but he sought it out "because it was mentioned they believe in modern prophets." He became a member almost as a reflex action. Soon he met Helga, who was sitting in the pew he chose that first Sunday, shy and grateful to be in the right place at last. He held her at the waist while they spoke with us. She looked into his eyes and smiled her warm smile. They were sealed in the Dallas temple a year earlier.

There were Avrahim Al-alamain and Cynthia de Torres-Obregon-Johannsen of Arabic and Syrian, Spanish, English and Dutch ancestry. Their conversion stories span a one hundred year history of half the known world and took over a week to relate — in English. Brother Norman Tiger, a 47-year old bachelor and third generation Mormon, had recently inherited a large llama ranch and was even more anxiously looking for a wife. The elderly Womacs, lifelong members, lived closer to the branch than anyone, in a home purchased for them by their surviving children. Sister Womac, in her eighties and hard of hearing, also suffered from Alzheimer' disease. Her husband cared for her lovingly and whispered the sacrament talks into her right ear so she wouldn't miss anything.

We met many other sweet and spiritual people that day and promised to visit and assist them all. Terry and Joanna Wolf were young, energetic working cowboys from West Texas who showed their horses all over the country. Terry told us he had never read the Doctrine and Covenants past Section One. He was waiting for the meaning of that amazing portion to sink deeply into his soul. We were charmed by Sister Delilah Parrey, my age, smart, sassy and well to do, a convert at twenty, with roots deep in Texas soil. She claimed membership in the sisterhood of the Daughters of the American Revolution.

"We fought in Texas, too, honey," she drawled, adjusting her expensive blouse. Her blonde pageboy was perfectly cut. It curled over the silk collar.

"You all need to know that even the south wanted peace and harmony in the Yewnited States. My granddaddy was a fighter, and his granddaddy before him? When I heard of Joseph Smith, living as he did in that cold country up east, a Yankee, well, I just sat down and said 'How can this book be true?' But it was and I knew it soon enough. Been a member, lo these many years. Relief Society president for five. I do shepherd the youth of this branch to Dallas every few months to do proxy baptisms. You all come over for Texas barbecue real soon, you heah?" Her smile disclosed perfect teeth.

"Texas barbecue? Does she marinate the meat? Does she make the pasta?" Sister DiNate asked me when we were alone. I told her I guessed we'd likely be served our ribs drenched in a strong barbecue sauce. Also lots of red beans and baked potatoes, probably with lots of cheese and chili.

"Ah," she said, nodding philosophically. "Maybe I fast that day."

There was well-mannered, shy Bud Meiers, a new member, formerly a Baptist and before that, southern Methodist. He was blonde and sweet, attractive in a southern way with his dark blue suit, French shirt cuffs and silken maroon tie. All the single sisters had their eye on him, but he seemed to be more interested in the priesthood and in teaching the youth.

"I taught in middle school," he said in that slow southern drawl that ends each sentence like a question.

"Teaching is my natural forte. I love this Gospel, you know what I mean? These kids need a real good teacher in this branch and I would sure like that calling?"

His blue eyes reminded me of open sky and his aftershave spoke to me of magnolias. He made a little bow to us and gently took our hands. That had me blushing right away, but Sister DiNate kept staring at him. So when he left I teased her about being used to dark, heavy Italian men who smelled of garlic, or the New England hard weather types who always wore windbreakers and heavy sheepskin boots. She put the fingers of her right hand together and bobbed them in the air.

"Always he is like that? So charming, like honey dripping? I make him a spicy spaghetti, then we see."

Things settled down promptly at nine. We were called to sit near the bishop on the stand. He brought the meeting brought to order and introduced us with gusto. After the sacrament was passed, it was time for testimonies. Everyone looked at us. Sister DiNate nudged me, I nudged her back. "Ah," she breathed and went to the podium.

"Buon giorno, brothers and sisters of this branch of Zion. Today my new sister, Sister Davis and me, we begin our mission here. We so happy to be here. We want to know you. I am Italian, from Barre, that's barr-ay, Vermont where there are big granite pits. Now the summers there are beautiful. I miss it very much. Never I have been here in your Texas — ah, south central Texas."

She paused to think of her next words. Faces were uplifted in expectation but Sister DiNate seemed to be searching within herself for something deeper; she was silent for a moment.

"This day I think of my familia coming from Italy. They left the beautiful Calabria, the farms and the oak forests, the Arno. The Ionian Sea they left, and their fishing for to come to America. We were Catholic. The missionaries found me in the snow and I got baptized. Then I met Joseph, a Catholic man, so we married by a priest in Catholic ceremony and then we marry again by a Mormon bishop. Joseph and me, we have six children."

Suddenly she stopped. I felt a sudden chill. Something inside her was fighting new tears.

"Excuse please, I have to stop. I think of my lovely boy, my young Joseph. He was sent to war." Sister DiNate gulped for control. She swung her head in a reflex motion and some hair loosened from its comb clip.

"My Joseph, he never returned to his mother. He is with his Father in heaven. I know, with Jesus Christ. His body they never found, but his spirit . . . that is with God." A sob escaped her throat. I choked up, too, hearing this information for the first time.

Her upturned palms lay upon the air. Her voice grew very soft. "My family is Catholic. If not for a miracle I would be still in Italy at the Mass. Now I take a mission. Why I go on a mission, leave my Vermont, my pasta, mia familia? My Father in heaven, he wants me, Sister DiNate, to be a missionary. Here I am."

Sister DiNate sat down heavily, wiping her eyes, and the congregation wiped theirs. I gave her shoulders a hug. The Spirit was very much a presence. Brother Womac was unable to whisper into his wife's ear until he had well cleared his throat. Bishop Brennan beamed his approval. Sister Parrey was whispering to Brother Tiger. Her laughter tinkled gently through the room. Sister DiNate remarked to me later that she could feel the congregation's love. I wanted to enjoy the moment, so I sat quietly a bit before rising to speak.

"Good morning, my brothers and sisters. I bring you greetings from Oregon. Being here among you in this warm southern climate has saved me from a cold, wet winter in the lush northwest." That brought a laugh.

As I stood acquainting the congregation with my life and times, I realized that we are each our own most knowledgeable genealogists. Every heart is a catalogue, every mind carries an unerasable record of its unique, changing past. Whose life does not, as it moves inexorably toward its fullness, draw a moving line of descent backward past children, partners, the bustle of time? We are living books of remembrances, collectors of the finer moments, but sadness can lurk in the best of times.

"I met Michael Davis one lucky day. He came from a family of welders and builders and he was an expert with tools, he could do anything in my eyes. We used to take trips across the country. One time we happened by a sign that pointed to Palmyra, New York. I was never raised with religion but I'd heard of the Mormon Church, so I suggested we see the Sacred Grove. In the Grove, something came toward me, some shining force. I fell to my knees. My head became light and I think I fainted for a moment right there in the brilliance. Michael had walked on ahead but he came running back. In that moment I saw our Savior's blazing white countenance and heard him speak to me as one speaks to another." I could see it all as I spoke, the blinding glare of whiteness before me, his kind, quiet voice speaking to my heart...

"How could a finer moment be possible? That experience transformed me. I soon joined the Church with Michael in tow. I am so grateful for our temple marriage."

As others came forward to bear their own sweet witness of Christ and his Church, memories of my last year with Michael flashed back to me — his illness, the hospital time, the final few months together.

"You're going to be an orphan," he teased me when we knew his life was ebbing away. "But it's only for a little while." At the last, Michael held me to him and we slept that way until the night air crept across the pillow and made him shiver. "All good things come together," he said in a whisper. "Aren't we a sure thing?"

Our closing hymn was "I Need Thee Every Hour", a favorite of mine and of our late prophet, President Howard W. Hunter, himself a man of heavy burden, but holy and at peace, as if his discerning eyes beheld that joyous Visage, finally but a breath away.

3 Dinner invitations and service calls were not long in coming to us. Members' homes were often miles away from anyone else, spread all over the county. Our gas bill tripled. Bambina soon needed a tune-up and oil change. I learned to milk cows, Sister DiNate got pretty good at working a lariat while singing Calabrian folk songs at the Wolf's "spread." On the day all our teaching appointments cancelled we utilized our time by practicing our missionary Discussions before Brother Tiger's llamas while he visited his mother in Austin. They were polite and appeared to consider our arguments.

Many of those we met were lifelong residents of the area, happy to fill us in on the weather patterns, the town's long history and where the best bargains were to be found. We learned about recent Texas political problems, other members, and regional gossip. We, in turn were diligent missionaries. We prayed and read with them. We helped them clean their barns and feed their livestock and baby-sat their family's children. When opportunities arose, we asked about their relatives, proselytized with their neighbors and arranged baptisms for eligible children of record. We were a patrol on the lookout for the untaught, the unwarned and not baptized.

We looked for them initially through membership's extended family and friends, doing our best to fellowship as many of the hundred and seventy branch members as we could locate. The flowers of summer came out to herald us as we drove our appointed rounds and blessed cool night covered them as we retraced the roads. Bambina became less forgiving of the potholes on the farm to market roads, while her sweaty occupants developed a deepening respect for "driving Texas" in 90%-plus humidity.

Few opportunities were missed in those first harried weeks as Sister DiNate and I felt the heavy mantle of living life "on the Lord's time." Thanks to the invaluable help of our sweet young Elders, the brethren and the branch presidency we cultivated a landscape of souls and fed each other in ways no mere bread could duplicate.

Almost imperceptibly, President Fowler's words of admonition became prophecy. There was little time to long for the virtues of Oregon. Letters from my companion's family in Vermont piled up on the dresser, to be read hastily before bed or saved for P-days. We discovered catfish, delicious and plentiful. Sister DiNate found macaroni to be quite tolerable when drenched in her homemade spaghetti sauce. We made do, as they say, in this quaint and sultry land of bluebells, oak groves and seemingly endless farmland.

"We Rodent Rooter patrol today," joked Sister DiNate after one long day of cleaning Sister Parrey's cupboards and setting mouse traps to catch the hungry little varmints after a particularly hard rain.

"We clean out Texas from the mice, save the carpets from the crumbs, sing the babies to sleep, mama mia! Where are the souls to baptize?"

"They'll come, they'll come," I tiredly reassured. We were taking rare advantage of lounging on our newly cleaned plaid couch. I reached for our burgeoning prayer list. "Maybe we'd better do more tracting in town. Those lucky Texans haven't had the joy of meeting us senior missionaries yet. We can try out some new opening lines."

"Sister Warner, she has a friend in the ward, a familia. But they not active. The teenage son, he tells the Warners he want to come back. He say we must come to his house, 10 a.m. We can to go tomorrow morning, yes?"

"I'll put it on our planner. Right now I'd love some hot chocolate, and our prayers await us . . . Sister, are you already praying or just falling asleep?"

4 I'd better warn you about Benny George Maloney, the only child of Pauline and Herman. Benny G loved rap music better than anything and he made it come alive walking through the dark green rooms of his parents' house. His face pushed forward in a downward slope. Full lips pursed to kiss the air, Benny G opened his black eyes wide while one hand grabbed a hip. The other was a spear aimed at his invisible audience.

"Slap. Yo. Do you read me? Huh? I'm a rappah! Come and hear me, rap, flap!" In all his eighteen years nothing had so stirred his young soul as the punctuated phrases that shot like ak-ak from "the lips of the hippest, like Ice T, like Rappah Man!"

His disapproving mother saw her son put goo in his brown hair every morning and coax the ends into spikes. She saw him put on his leather jacket dangling with silver chains and 1" brass spikes all over the back of it and she complained to us that he had become a living porcupine. But she couldn't laugh, because guilt for raising him outside the Church ate at her daily. Pauline remembered Benny G as a child — he had a smile like an angel and a gentle demeanor. She'd read him to sleep with the Psalms. Over the years he memorized many of them and made up tunes to the meter of the words. Pauline shook her head. She mourned him and his passing.

"Once, long, long ago, I believed he had promise. I saw in him a disciple, a disciplined follower of the Savior."

All of that was absent now. Benny G was a child of the world. His round teenaged face was host to a nose that lifted itself into a wide-nostril snub above a rosy, pimply skin. His upper lip and lower face had sprouted what looked to me like prairie dirt. The letters C-O-O-L rose off his chest and cut across his thick neck in bold tattooing just above his shirt collar and his "once sweet" tenor voice had taken on a hoarse, sensuous throb.

"That's like, how Ice T sounds, man. Cool!"

Benny G was a clown. Stumbling around the living room and through the kitchen with Walkman wires coming out of his ears he resembled nothing so much as a Jersey steer gamboling through a pasture. Pauline was grateful that they lived thirty miles from the nearest LDS church where she was brought up. His father, Herman had never joined any church, but he had no objection to anyone else's membership. Herman took life easy, knowing that it was good and that he was essentially power-less to change his fate. His son's antics amused him. Benny G had been baptized in the other end of that valley when just eight, but he took to following his father into the bars around the lake near their trailer home, just to be around dad. He still did that and they would help each other through the weeds above the lake front toward home under a friendly moon, happily singing whatever they'd heard on the jukebox that night. If he could, Benny G would try to teach his father to rap.

Pauline was a victim of a bad back and migraines. Much of her days were spent in her dark bedroom with ice packs. She didn't seem to fit in the picture of a family setting and she had no control over the lives of her husband or son. They just all seemed to go their own ways and meet once in a while in the middle. That's where we found them asleep that next morning at 10, in the living room. Benny G finally answered our knocks. His eyes were bloodshot and he needed a shower.

"Hey, is it morning? What can I do for you . . . ah, sisters?"

A blanket hung from his shoulders like a crumpled cape. He was star-ing blearily at my badge, his lower lip extended in puzzlement. Catching the cue, I said

"Good morning. My name is Sister Davis and this is Sister DiNate We're missionaries from The Church of Jesus Christ of Latter-day Saints here to see you — "

"Latter-day Saints," Benny G said it with us like it was a rap duet. 'Right on time, it must be ten. Sisters D and D, don't tarry. Come on in and missionary.' I'm Benny G, been expecting you!"

He motioned us inside their spacious mobile home. Instinctively, I hunched against my jacket, not knowing what to expect. Behind me I heard DiNate's low, mournful wail. MTC never told us we'd have times like these! But dutifully we stepped inside.

It was dark and smelled of liquor. Drapes on the windows were pulled shut. On the couch near us lay Herman Maloney, Benny G's father, cov-ered by his jacket and still asleep, snoring gently, an empty highball glass on the table near him. Pauline, at the other end of the couch, straightened her red hair and summer pantsuit and pulling on her low heels in obvi-ous embarrassment she quickly stood up, but she tripped in her shoes and fell back onto the couch. Benny G rushed over to retrieve her. They wobbled there together, trying to face us bravely as if we were the advance cadre for a visit from the First Presidency and they had been caught with all their lamps trimmed. I stifled a laugh, extending my hand to Pauline first and then to Benny G. Her hand was cool, but Benny G put a heavy, sweaty grip on my palm.

"How're ya doin'", he said with feigned interest, moving to shake DiNate's hand. She gave him a "Ciao." A smile froze in her wide, dark eyes. Pauline was trying to wake Herman and pull open the drapes.

"I'm sorry," she said with a self-conscious laugh. "We forgot the time. Do have a seat?" We sat near the couch. Herman turned over in half-sleep, his back to us, and resumed his snoring. Pauline swore beneath her breath and vaulted his leather jacket toward his head. It was not a Kodak moment.

"Maybe this is not the time," I began, trying to relieve the obvious strained atmosphere. "We were told that someone in this family wanted to reactivate in the Church."

"That would be me," Benny G spoke up and he settled himself and his mother again on their couch. "I used to go, you know, now and then, but, well, school and all, and lots of things, and I stopped going, but I'd like to learn again, I mean, if you all could teach me or give me a book to read or somethin', you know what I mean?"

"Do you have a Book of Mormon?"

"Yeah, I do, somewhere, packed it away. Want me to look for it?" He wasn't the least repentant, but he was trying.

We agreed, and while he rustled around in his room, Pauline fixed us cold orange juice. Herman continued to snore blissfully.

It was the knock at the door that changed everything.

"Would you get that?" Pauline called from the sink.

DiNate opened it. There stood a girl in her teens. She wore a plain, flowered, long waisted dress that showed her plumpness, but shone with cleanliness. Short reddish brown hair, unevenly cut was brushed carefully back of her ears. She wore tennis shoes without socks and her ankles were scarred from walking through brush. She carried no purse or jacket, but in her small hand she had a bouquet of summer wildflowers. I had the quick impression that there was no darkness in her, as if she was glowing from inside her dress.

"Hi, I'm Carla. Are you the missionaries? Oh, I see you are. I'm Carla." She laughed at herself. "Benny G told me you'd be here today. I came to see you, too."

It was her eyes that held us, I remember. Like her thick brows they were brown, but of a rich dark umber tint, flecked with deeper brown and black. Wide-set and framed with thick lashes her eyes were like precious stones on view as they rested calmly on each person like a blessing. They studied, they seemed to penetrate substance, and they appeared to look upon the world with a languid clarity and an unmistakable happiness.

We welcomed her inside. I gave her my seat. Pauline came in with the juice. Carla smilingly handed Pauline the flowers.

"Oh, how sweet, Carla! Have you met the sisters?" She read from our badges: "Ah... Davis and duh Naytay, is it? Carla is Benny's little friend and she's come to hear you today. Oh, Herman, honestly."

Herman had snored himself awake. Seeing Carla he blushed. "Carla," he said and then quickly rose and walked toward the bathroom. "Shower," he mumbled beneath his breath.

Benny came back empty handed and noticeably subdued.

"Guess I've lost —" Oh, hi Carla. You look pretty today. So bright and all." He blushed. She blushed. I checked our planner and sighed. This was going to be a long morning . . .

But something told me to look carefully at this new arrival. There was an electricity in her demeanor that seemed to pull one closer. She smiled sweetly and easily in our presence. Her lovely eyes followed Benny G like a child finding chocolate, but he was too full of himself to notice.

Eventually, she settled herself and began to tell us her story. Jeanine Carla McCoy was sixteen then, delivered by her mother when only ten to her maternal grandmother, an aged Missouri widow from the remote no-man's-land "apiece" west of the Arkansas border. This woman, cut from poor cloth in old Ozark shantytown tradition and abandoned with seven children in the prime of her womanhood, had long since decided to obey her own persuasions. She fed her sorrow with malt liquor and counted the hard days with Old Gold straights and scratched old 33-rpm recordings of the Smoky Mountain Boys. But though now sick and embittered, she felt obliged to take this simple child in her home so that her oldest daughter would have an opportunity to recover from her marriage of failed purpose and regain some financial footing.

Sandra, Carla's mother, 35 and nearly penniless, was separating her life from a man eleven years her senior who had gone broke as a farmer and taken up his own father's habit of looking for love among the town's red light habitue's. Sandra packed her few belongings, begged her mother to take Carla "for a small spell" and with rushed good-byes moved with her infant son out of state to find work and a better life. She left no forwarding address. But much to Carla's and her grandmother's sadness and loss, Sandra never came back. The old woman and her granddaughter were thus thrown together and forced to accustom themselves to each other, but it was an uneasy alliance.

Mrs. Sloan lived with Carla in a dilapidated 1960's trailer home two miles east of Benny G's place. The trailer was unfortunately situated in the low brushy land near the lake. It had to be raised up from the ground on boards so the sump from the lake wouldn't rot the rickety foundation. Carla had a room in the back that a neighbor had added on for them, but he'd used wet pine, so it smelled badly and leaked. She was always cold there. "I'm used to it," she shrugged. She had long ago settled in to being left behind and forgotten, training herself to endure what little would come her way. Little more than a transient poverty was all she'd ever known.

DiNate looked at me and we found ourselves exchanging searching looks. Could it be that this guileless child was the one we had been sent to find? Within me a new feeling started, that of a hunger to teach her, a need for hurry, to cut her out from the pack. Like a runner bearing a precious new secret that could only be imparted to a chosen few, I wanted to tell her of Christ. I felt a sudden urgency to place for the first time in her innocent hands those anciently revealed, precious words of life and discover with her all over again their inspired messages. I wanted to see her eyes light with that diamond fire of first discovery of truth that shocks the body and spirit like oncoming headlights. As she smiled at us I imagined tears of gratitude flowing from those cedar eyes down her soft young face.

In my excitement I looked again at my companion. She had moved closer to the girl, gently patting her hand and cooing softly.

"Bella Bambina, bella." Her eyes were fixed upon Carla like a miner sighting a vein of yellow ore shining through miles of powdery gloom.

But we had to move slowly. We asked the child more about her home life. Carla told us she had to care for her sick "granmamau", using the Southern "family" term for one's grandmother and heavily emphasizing the -mam part of the word.

"She's hardly able any more. Suffers from that cough, I think it's terberker-losis, but she won't give 'em up."

Cigarettes were the poison Carla referred to, and the beer and coffee the woman drank all day didn't compensate. Still, Carla was clean and looked well. She sat with Benny G on the couch, smiling into his eyes and touching lightly the brass studs on the sleeve of his jacket. But Benny G pretended not to notice. Carla went on.

"Granmamau's real sick now, can't do much. I look out for her, do her wash, feed her when she can't get out of bed, you know?" She paused and looked sadly down at her hands. Her young mouth pursed. "She says she wants to die. Don't know who'll take me then . . . she's very hard on me, but it's all I know anymore." Much more softly she whispered, "Wish I could get married."

DiNate started to ask a question but before she got three words out, Benny G jumped up as if on cue.

"Look here. I have fifteen minutes before the game." His eyes lit up. He stared at me. "We're all big baseball fans here. You want to watch with us?"

"No," DiNate almost growled, barely taking her eyes from Carla's sweet face. We missionaries, we teach. Yes, we help you, Benny, but we don't do baseball, eh." She began to unzip her scripture case, not looking up.

Benny G seemed only mildly deflated. Then he looked at Carla like a new idea had hit him.

"I know! You can teach her, that's it. She really wants to learn about Jesus, don't you, Carla? Tell them, it's okay, what you told me? Don't be shy about it. You all can even study in my room." He backed up toward the TV across the room, out of the light, waiting to see if his artful dodge would work.

Gentle Carla blushed again and fumbled with her hands for a moment.

"I, well, see, my granmamau won't let you come over . . . She . . . well . . . she hates Mormons, but Benny G says you have the truth about Jesus. I want to know the truth about Jesus. Don't care what your church is called, as long as it can teach me about him." She said "Jesus" like "Cheesus" and blushed again, but there was no mistaking her sincerity in expressing a cherished longing she'd probably held secret, afraid and unwilling to share it with her "granmamau" or anyone else, until now.

Sister DiNate shook her head affirmatively in obvious agreement.

"We teach you, Carla. Your friend is right, we have the truth about Jesus and his Church. We tell it to you. When you want to start?"

Sister DiNate found her planner and hoisted a new pen. She looked at Carla, then at my own eagerness, bobbing her head up and down in pleasure and smiling for the first time since the day began.

Carla's serious eyes searched ours for the entrance to a path long ago chosen. As they brightened her whole attention seemed to rivet upon a force directly in front of her.

"Now," she said with a mature sureness in her voice that I will never forget. "I want to learn right now." She rose and turned toward Benny G's room.

Sister DiNate and I followed her in and settled ourselves. Was she as eager to begin as we were? I wondered what testimony she already possessed.

"Carla, we are so happy to teach you the Gospel," I began. Before we open with a prayer I must ask — what do you know of Heavenly Father?"

She was silent a moment, looking past us through the blinds that barred the window light. The temperature outside was rising and it looked like there would be no wind to ease the sultry humidity. But our day was turning out to be perfect.

"Heavenly Father is my only joy," this child said softly in her southern drawl, her untinted lips trembling, fierce with pride. The passion in her voice made my throat catch. "He is my only, only joy."

6 We taught Carla the First Discussion that day and the Second Discussion the following week. She met us at Benny G's on that Sunday evening, walking the two miles from her home. She handed each of us a colorful bouquet of wildflowers she'd picked as she walked. The three of us sat outside listening to mockingbirds and slapped at the mosquitoes tasting our skin. But she was thirsty for the Spirit, hungry for the meat of the gospel. She asked many questions. We hardly acted as teachers with her, for she so readily accepted what we told her that the mere explanation of sacred concepts and principles served almost as reminders. Her serious eyes mirrored the solemnity of 2 Nephi, narrowed and focused upon us as we quoted from Isaiah. Many times the tears came down her cheeks to her plain dress before she noticed to wipe them away.

We noticed eventually that Carla would not read the scriptures, either to herself or out loud. She sweetly encouraged us to read to her, not once but repeatedly, not a sampling only, as was normal, but all that we could summon from memory and from the Bible index.

At first we accepted it, glad enough for her passionate interest, but her reticence bothered me. "Carla, when we leave you with reading assignments, do you earnestly study your Book of Mormon?"

Carla blushed and looked down at the book we had placed in her hands to follow along as we read. Then, with a deep sigh, she gave up the lie.

"Guess I can't fake it any more. The thing is, I can't read, Sister Davis. I never was able to stay in one school very long and I just didn't learn to sound the letters right . . . I don't know how the "e's" are supposed to sound, or how to say most of the "u's and i's". Granmamau tried to help when she got me, but I never really, well, I just don't understand without sounding out every word . . . and by then I forget what it's about . . . I'm sorry. I should have told you right away, but . . . I'm really sorry . . . How am I gonna learn this book?"

And her tears of sorrow fell all over Moroni 7:33 which I had just begun. And Christ hath said: If ye will have faith in me ye shall have power to do whatsoever thing is expedient in me.

Then I remembered something I'd heard at Senior MTC. There have been many occasions where people have learned to read by using the Book of Mormon and simultaneously listening to it on taped cassettes. I mentioned it to her and she looked at me in disbelief.

"The Book of Mormon is on tape? Wow, that would solve it for sure. But how can I get it?"

We assured her we could work that part out. I knew of a set of tapes at the branch president's home. He'd lend it to her and we could give her programmed reading so she could hear the lessons and follow along with the book. It would take time but she'd grasp the lessons and the continuity of the scriptures while learning the words. We could even help her to master the scriptures as she learned to identify the words. I was really grateful for that program.

But the biggest hindrance was yet to come. We had challenged Carla to be baptized and she'd agreed, but there was the issue of her grandmother. Carla had told Mrs. Sloan that she was taking lessons from Mormon missionaries.

"She got really angry at me, but she didn't say I couldn't see you any more. She says you can teach me a little, but I can't get baptized 'cause I'm only sixteen." Carla looked as if she was going to cry again.

"You can't come over, either. She doesn't want you on her territory. I'm sorry, I really am, but she just doesn't like Mormons, I don't know why, she won't tell me. She just says it's her private business."

DiNate and I thought long and hard about that one as we drove home after dropping Carla off near her grandmother's place. This child was "golden" and she'd readily agreed to be baptized. How were we going to get around the grandmother? Because Carla was not yet eighteen, we needed her parent or guardian's written permission to baptize her a member of the Church. Was Mrs. Sloan legally liable for Carla? And where were her parents?

"Well, we can go see that woman anyway and have a talk," DiNate offered. "Maybe she tell us what's eating her. Maybe we all talk it over."

"If we can even get in the house. Remember Carla said we can't go on her grandmother's property. I guess the worst she can do is order us away. I wonder what she has against Mormons?"

"Must to be very heavy. Maybe we go anyway and I bring her pasta. How she can turn down hot Italian pasta?"

Instead we decided first to pray and fast about it before pursuing it further. Carla had been discovering her love for the Savior, it was a revelation to watch. She had a new, strong testimony that we represented his church and she wanted to know what it looked like. Did we need permission to take her there? Surely the branch president could help us.

President Howard owned a recycling plant. We found him hard at work sorting and loading onto trucks before continuing his route around town. He greeted us joyfully.

"So! You found me at work! Great day, got to gather all we can before the sun sets. What can I do for you sweet sisters?" He made a little bow to us and we went inside his office. We told him of finding Carla and her growing love for the gospel. When we mentioned her desire to be baptized his eyes began to tear. By the time we finished our story he'd already fished a Book of Mormon out of his desk and turned its pages to Alma 32.

"You have found a soul who has lived in poverty of life but is rich of spirit," he began. "This sweet child has had the Holy Ghost testify to her. He has brought her perhaps the only peace and true love she has ever known, and now she hungers for more. We must not deny her that precious gift of life that she so richly deserves."

He touched a scripture with his thick, scarred fingers and read to us.

"16. Therefore, blessed are they who humble themselves without being compelled to be humble; or rather, in other words, blessed is he that believeth in the word of God, and is baptized without stubbornness of heart . . .

"Now, sisters, this child must be taught and baptized. We must find a way to make that happen. There is something in the grandmother's past that is preventing her from accepting responsibility, something left unfinished in her life. She has fear for the child, but perhaps it really goes much deeper than we think. In every mission there are problems, hurdles that look difficult, some even hopeless. But nothing is impossible with God. Faith. Yours, mine, Carla's, and the faith of this branch will have a lot to do with the results we get. Look here at verse 41. 'But if ye will nourish the word . . . by your faith with great diligence, and with patience, looking forward to the fruit thereof, it shall take root.' Now, that is what you must do. I agree with your idea of fasting and praying, but then you must take action. We are here to war upon Satan and deprive him of his prey. Let us offer up a prayer at this time."

And filled with the Spirit we prayed there in President Howard's tiny office. Though we still had no answers we were full of hope. As we began our fast at that time, we asked Heavenly Father for revelation and the courage of Alma and Helaman. Oh, Lord, she is only one woman, I thought. But without persuasion and a change of heart, she might as well be an army. As I rose from my knees I was quietly corrected.

"You are my soldiers," the voice said to my heart. "In my Father's army only the righteous finally triumph."

7 We stood very uncertainly on the wooden step outside Mrs. Sloan's trailer. I looked at DiNate. Her mouth was set, her eyes ready for battle. She'd even worn her largest silver hair clip, like a back-up shield hidden among the thick waves of black and gray. My own heart was beating loudly. We'd prayed, fasted and prayed some more. Here was the acid test.

We found the rusty trailer again, following the trail of Texas soap bush that stretched its stout, crooked branches into the dirt road that lined the lake. Weeds almost hid the front path. We carefully picked our way across slabs of broken concrete tiles to the old grained wooden door. DiNate offered to knock. No one answered. I knocked, harder. In another moment the door opened a crack. A small, very thin woman peered up at us. Mrs. Sloan. She wore a smudged yellow scarf around her head. The sickening smell of frying grease mingled with the wheaty essence of stale beer and nicotine. It wafted out to greet us. The woman opened the door further. With a bony hand she held a cigarette at cheek level. The whites of her eyes had a yellow tint. She focused on our name badges. I found myself staring at her nose, thin and long, but also somewhat hooked. The impression was that of a hungry bird sighting new prey. It frightened me and I took a step backward.

"Whatdaya want here?" Hard green eyes stared at me and at DiNate, who was rooted.

"We missionaries, Church of Jesus Christ of Latter-day Saint."

"I know who ya are. Ya want Carla, don't you? Well, she ain't coming out. She's busy."

"Mrs Sloan," I tried in my softest voice, "we are so glad to finally meet you. Carla has told us that we might come to ask your help."

It didn't work. Her jaw softened barely a muscle, but hard glints of emerald fire bored into mine.

"Look. I don't know you people, but Carla's joined half a dozen church-es in her few years. I know what you Mormons believe, I grew up among ye. When this child's mother brought her to me she didn't have nobody else. Carla's slow, easy trusting and gets in lots of trouble if she ain't handled right. Carla cain't read, ya know. Did she tell ya? She cain't think like she should, she's simple. I got to protect her and protect her I will, from you Mormons and everyone else in this lousy world. Now get off my steps." The door slammed in our faces.

DiNate looked at me in shock, then with great deliberation turned as if in slow motion and knocked again.Surprisingly, it was opened. Mrs. Sloan looked like she would gladly bite us. DiNate said quickly,

"We understand you love Carla. You don't want anyone taking her advantage. But Carla has good mind. She wants to see our church. Now if you want to make her so angry that maybe she runs away to see it, you forbid her. But we will love and protect her, too. We must to ask your permission she can see our church on Sunday. Then she'll be thankful to you, you'll see, it's true, e` vero."

It all came tumbling out, but it was just enough to catch the woman off guard. She stared intently at Sister DiNate and just at that moment Carla came to the door, her childlike body moving the old woman a little off her stance.

"Hi, Sister Davis. Sister DiNate, thought it was you."

Ignoring her grandmother Carla extended her hand to each of us and we shook it with relief. She blushed a little and turning to the woman fuming silently beside her she said sweetly

"Granmamau, please let them come on in. I want them to see my little flower garden out back. I can pick them a bouquet. Please, they mean no harm."

Mrs. Sloan shot us a mean glance and then aimed another at Carla. Her cigarette had burned itself down to her fingers. She threw it out the door, between us. Her look softened slightly, but she moved sideways, forcing her granddaughter backward just enough. In her voice was new honey.

"Now, Carla, I've talked to you about these things. You're too young to know what you want. These people will teach you things that ain't true, no offense to you ladies, so nicely dressed and all, but, honey, you just don't know these folk and the others like 'em that're always comin' to our door. Now your mama —"

"Mamau's gone, and she's not coming back. She's left us all behind, you know it and I know it. These people are my friends. They're helping me learn English. I'm almost eighteen and —"

"Two more years, child! You can count! Then ye kin decide for yourself, but 'til then I decide for ye. I got legal custody, remember? Now back to your room, young 'un, and let these ladies be on their way to spread their poison elsewhere. We've talked on this before."

"Granmamau, please let them in. I want them here!" Carla's voice rose in helpless terror. What did she have to fight this woman with? "Please!"

Mrs. Sloan looked at her, then turned to look up at us, her thin little body shook with righteous anger. She smelled of worldly poisons. Her lips curled in the throes of a grimace, but those eyes, wary as ever, held fierce triumph. DiNate straightened her back in protest. I felt only doom because Carla's twisted look said it all. Her face dark and full of pain, her mouth a tremor. Surely that conversation with her grandmother had with small variation taken place many times before and Carla must have expected it with every move she made toward freedom. She was crying bitterly now. I reached for her. Mrs. Sloan pushed her backward into the room as she sobbed, and two of the Lord's missionaries cried silently with her as the heavy, rotting wooden door slammed again with finality. We were shut out, but Carla was the real victim. She had become marooned.

❧

Deep in pits of gloom we drove slowly by Benny G's place, not consciously looking for comic relief, but hoping that somehow we might discover within his strangely bouyant personality a key, a secret way back into Carla's life that only he could provide. But no one was at home and we headed with a leaden reluctance back to town for a couple of hours of tracting a new housing development.

DiNate was silent, but she was steaming like a potful of pasta. My own thoughts were tangled up in frustration and impinging despair when we swerved to miss an armadillo scurrying across the heated road.

"That's us," DiNate fumed. "We're like that thing in the road and everyone moves around us when they see us coming."

"Not everyone. Carla came out to meet us, remember? It's her grandmother who's trying to stop progress in that house."

"She hide that child behind her. Why you think she hate us? Do we smell, are we criminals?"

I tried not to laugh at DiNate's dramatics, but neither of us were used to double-barreled rejection. I wondered if she had a shotgun and if she'd shoo us off her porch with it, or maybe shoot us.

"We'll work it out, we've got resources. We need to think. We need to go home, put our heads together and scheme, okay?"

"Scheme, schmeme. Mama mia, we got to ask for help!"

We pulled into the housing development and parked, readying our packs for a new tracting episode. But as we prayed for success here our hearts were elsewhere and our busy little brains were hot with the fever of challenge.

8 I was somewhere in my car with Michael, driving the cold, broad beach fronts of the Oregon coast when the phone call came. It was Carla, bringing me back to Texas at 2 a.m.

"Sister Davis, I'm so sorry. I know it's late but I had to talk to you. I can't sleep, been listenin' to the tapes you got me. I'm reading along with the book, learnin' to read, you know, finally learning, and when I do I'm goin' to that library in Fairfield and I'm gonna get every book they got and read 'em all!"

"Carla, honey, it's 2 a.m. We were sleeping here. And aren't you worried about waking your grandmother?"

"She can't hear me in here, in my room. We got a long cord on this phone since I got here. I apologize for her, she just hates Mormons and other folks full of their religions."

"Why? Why does she hate Mormons?"

"It's when she was young. Granmamau's from Missouri, the real poor part, below the Breaks. Her mama's brother Everett was Mormon, but they was never close and they used to fight all the time about money for drinking and such. They was poor folk. He was real strict, like in the book, that Nephi? Uncle Everett took over raising granmamau after her mama died of a sickness. He used to catch her out smoking and drinking beer but she'd fight him every time. He and his wife made her go to church every week to learn the Mormon ways. She hated it there but they made her go."

"It was wrong to push her into it."

"Yes, ma'am. She ran away 'bout every day, but Uncle Everett knew the whole town, he always found her. She wanted to be on her own, but she was just twelve when her mama died, so she had to listen to Uncle Everett and go to church."

"What was so bad about that?"

She hated everybody there, thought they was a cult, a lot of fakes. Says they all hated her and wouldn't come near her. She finally did run off at sixteen, to Arkansas where she met Granpa Don. He wanted to come here to Texas, so they moved so he could fish and hunt.

"She was the age you are now . . . I don't suppose Granpa Don was LDS?"

"No, ma'am, might he was a Pentecost. But he didn't practice and she didn't care, neither. They just started having babies. It made her real sick and she blamed Uncle Don for goin' off now and again and leavin' her alone with all of them. Finally one day, he just left . . . that was a long time ago but she ain't never forgiven him."

"I'm sorry. She's had a very hard life."

"She says her life is junk and she hates anyone trying to tell her different. She thinks I don't want to protect myself."

"From being unhappy, Carla, or from becoming like her?"

"Don't know, Sister Davis, I guess just trouble and having lots of kids. All her kids have run off. She don't hear from 'em."

"How do you feel about your life? Do you still want to learn the gospel?

Carla sighed heavily on the other end of the line.

"Oh, yes, ma'am. I want to learn more than ever. I'm listenin' to those tapes you gave me and reading along in the book. Things I need to ask you about . . . I'm so lonely here . . . could you give me a lesson on the phone? She won't know, she's asleep."

But we couldn't really teach on the phone. I wanted to talk with our mission president before any further lessons were given, considering Mrs. Sloan's admonition to us. I told Carla to be brave and have faith.She said she'd call every night until we saw her again and could free her to come to church with us.

"I have faith because I know the Lord wants me baptized into his Church. Don't give up on me, Sister Davis, you hear? Don't you all give up on poor Carla."

❧

But we were learning that missionaries don't give up, they just get busier. A hectic two weeks followed, full of appointments and missionary meetings. Most nights we had no time to cook or even to accept dinner invitations. We learned to make friends with the local 7-11's muffin rack and dairy case. Referrals led us everywhere. Bambina took us through the verdant hills past fat, varicolored livestock, sleek goats and maybe all the sheep in America. There was little time for deep contemplation of the wonders before us, but Carla's plight was ever with us. We whizzed across sparkling streams alive with fish and fishermen, climbed oak forested hill paths dark with overgrowth. We bounced across old wooden bridges bleached with age and found roads known intimately by brown bear and deer.

The world was full of summer light and shadow, and promise beckoned us forward. DiNate serenaded them all loudly with her favorite Verdi and to the overwhelming starry exhibitions of evening she dedicated a throbbing and moving Wagner. We had to stay busy to keep the swelter from overtaking us. We hunted out the curious, waited upon the indecisive, tried to edify the hungry and gratefully taught the faithful, until my treasured cool memories of being drenched in gray, cold Oregon rain were overtaken by endless sweaty treks beneath the unrelenting sun that made the land steam like a jungle.

And every night we received our awaited call from faithful Carla who was excited by her new discoveries of scripture. Her lonely spirit poured itself out to whoever answered the phone. The faith-promoting scriptures in Alma 32 became her favorite and she was working on reading them without assistance from the tapes. The book of Jacob stirred her deeply. She cried as she read, then laughed at herself.

Sister DiNate and I took turns as her lifelines to the outside world, because after returning from school, Carla was not allowed out of the house again that day. Mrs. Sloan, afraid her granddaughter would sneak away to Benny G's or arrange to meet us somewhere, would not relent. Discussion Three would have to wait upon divine intervention, it seemed. We wore out our knees asking for that blessing. I admit that at times I felt sure we'd never get that chance, but Carla never lost hope and her sweet insistence became like bread and we all partook.

9 I told DiNate as we dressed for church the following week that Sunday mornings are always promising when you're a missionary on your way to church. The sacrament beckons first, like a newly furrowed field, ready for planting. I close my eyes in prayer and imagine the Lord walks among us, collecting the repentant tears of the faithful.

"These are seeds of blessings to come," he explains as we contemplate his sacrifices in our behalf. "These few precious drops are mine to plant and they add nourishment to your eternity."

Friendly faces always offer a sweet fruit here in this, the Lord's garden of the faithful, but it is the investigator with the searching look that fills our time in church with increased hope and we hunters of the searching spirit are trained to instinctively look for them.

We arrived at church early, but this morning only familiar sights greeted us. Sister Parrey sat bright and gracious in mid-chapel. Her silver bracelets made a light jangle, their gleam calling attention to her svelte gray summer suit. She beckoned us to sit with her. Immediately her fragrant cologne wafted past me.

"Ah'll be in Dallas next week, you know, on business and then temple work. Ah do love that city, so much to do and no relief from the heat, but then, seeing my little ranch again after all that noisy traffic? Honey, there's no place like home. Who are you all working with these days?"

We shared with her a little of Carla's plight. Sister Parrey was attentive. Her interest increased noticeably when we told her about her the late night phone calls.

"Why, you poor things don't get your proper rest. That poor girl, what can we do to help her? She needs to be to church!"

Sister Parrey presided over a small, busy horse ranch about twenty miles south of Carla's place and she knew all the members within radius of the lake. While we talked her hazel eyes took on a mischievous glint and I couldn't help thinking she was up to something, but then the meeting began and she whispered only,

"Honey, I sure hope you can figure something out. Why, that old granmamau of hers could use a good ol' fashion spankin'!"

❦

Brother Tiger was on the stand extolling the virtues of longsuffering patience when DiNate, sitting on the aisle, gasped audibly in Italian Beside her in a wide pink bundle stood our Carla, dressed in a too-short, pink taffeta dress with pink tatting around the short sleeves and hem. It might have come from a garage sale. A floppy old straw hat hid her red hair, and white heeled shoes with black scuff marks across them held her scarred, stockingless feet. Her white-gloved hands gripped a brown clutch purse to her chest and her round face was almost colorless. At once I felt her painfully shy self-consciousness . . . and her courage. Her eyes darted around the room, taking in everything.

"Carla," DiNate and I said at once, pulling her down, making a seat between us. "What are you doing here!"

She gulped, dropped her purse and banged her head on the seat in front of her reaching for it, whispering frantically.

"I ran away. She went to the store and I hitched a ride on the highway. Had to come to church, couldn't wait no longer. Walked the last mile, I got so lost."

She was still huffing with exertion. People turned to look at her. Brother Tiger lost his train of thought and stared, too, until President Howard cleared his throat a couple of times.

Carla seemed to wither with the sudden attention, so I put my arm around her and DiNate softly consoled her. We sat that way throughout the service, our minds working it all over, but by the closing song our little charge had calmed and seemed to delight in the music, even attempted some of the words. She had a sweet soprano voice I thought would fit nicely into the branch's small choir. Silently I thanked Heavenly Father for bringing her to us.

Well, everyone wanted to meet Carla, who had removed her gloves and hat at my urging. They crowded around her, smiling as they recognized a golden discovery. We introduced her to most of the regular members who complimented her on her dress, her hat and smile and extended their hands in fellowship. Carla had recovered most of her self-assurance, giggling and gracious, she kept throwing me happy glances. President Howard came over to grip her hand and give it a vigorous shake.

"So you're the girl who lives by the lake! Welcome to our branch. Say, I'd like to get to know you a little better. Stop by my office after church, will you?" He caught our eyes.

Carla blushed red and looked at the floor.

"I — I'll have to get home 'fore I'm really missed. Maybe just for a minute?"

"We'll bring her," I promised, trying to figure out how to get her home in time to avoid a confrontation with her grandmother. As it turned out, the problem solved itself when the Werners volunteered. They lived only five miles north of her home and were delighted to get better acquainted. She carefully asked them to drop her off some yards from her place and they wisely agreed.

I will never forget that first time with Carla at church. She seemed to be in love. Gospel Essentials class was a time of wide-eyed discovery. She became completely engrossed. DiNate and I pointed out passages to her in our books. Shyly she asked questions, nodded enthusiastically at the answers as if she anticipated them. When a point was made she'd lean forward, giving it all her attention, then sit back dreamy-eyed, her eyes seeming to focus inward. Many times she sighed and smiled happily and tears of joy gathered in her tawny eyes. Truly, she was being fed exactly what she needed.

She was the center of attention in Relief Society. Sisters Werner and Parrey took her from us and put her with them. Others gathered around. Carla was like a magnet, the more she smiled and laughed, shining her lights upon the other sisters, the more energy and light seemed to emanate from the group. Even the lesson that hour was more spirited than usual.

"Carla, she's the life of the party today," DiNate boasted to me. "Only I hope her grandmother don't kill her when she gets home."

"It will work out," I consoled my anxious partner. "When Mrs. Sloan sees her walk in with that Sunday outfit, she'll be angry, but it'll be too late by then. I have a feeling Carla can handle her grandmother pretty well sometimes, don't you? I mean, she's had a lot of time to learn how."

Sister DiNate shrugged, no doubt recalling our recent experience at Mrs. Sloan's front door. We watched Carla's bright face so full of happiness as the lesson ended. Then we took her to meet with the branch president. He gently closed us out of the room. When Carla emerged twenty minutes later she was all smiles and tears.

"He told me I can get baptized soon as granmamau allows, and she can come see him or he'll go to her. Ain't that wonderful? He'd go see her? But she won't allow it, I know. She hates Mormons with —"

DiNate interrupted. "We know, we know, don't remind me. Don't worry, Carla. You go home and talk again your grandmother. You tell her you want this to happen, yes? Can she deny you forever?"

That was the question everything hung on, it hit home and stayed in our thoughts as we hugged Carla goodbye. For once she looked more doubtful than joyful as she left with the Werners.

"The Lord is on the case," I reflected to DiNate, watching them drive out of the church lot. "He'll make a way, somehow, someday..."

"Si, e`vero, but what year? What if we transferred first? Who will love her like we do? She's like a little daughter, you know?" DiNate's brow was furrowed with love and concern.

"Hope," I said. "Faith, lots more prayer, and hope. I guess this is a trial of our faith, too. The Lord will do the rest. Remember what our mission president told us? 'Plan on very few transfers.'"

I smiled reassuringly at my companion, hoping she didn't know me well enough to discern my own growing anxiety. Here appeared to be no solution. What was the key that finally would open the door?

There is an old saying in Italian, my dear companion used to tell me, that when something wonderful is about to happen the Lord sends a sparrow to tell us of it. Or, she offered, it could be a pigeon or a dove. After a moment she admitted that in ancient legend a crow had been seen delivering a flowering tree branch. I wondered about crows in ancient Italy and asked if she hadn't confused that story with the one about Noah sending out a dove to find dry land, but DiNate insisted on her version. Did we Americans have any such legends here, she wanted to know? All I could think of was the old ruse that good news calls you up on the telephone, while Western Union always brings the opposite luck. Now, of course, there's e-mail and web sites.

"And then the Gospel," she said triumphantly. "Remember the day you were handed the Book of Mormon? Wasn't that the good news day?"

She had me there. I was in fact holding my copy, reading out of Moroni 7 where we are reminded that we shall be known by our works and the manner in which we offer of ourselves, be it with real intent or superficially.

Carla had just called to tell us that her granmamau was loudly upset when the child returned from church. Mrs. Sloan's punishment was to immediately confine her granddaughter to the house for a week, no school, no walks, and if any Mormons came around their place they could expect to be shot with Mrs. Sloan's old squirrel gun that she kept by the front door, probably just for such occasions, I thought ruefully. Well, we'd all expected more trouble and we weren't left disappointed.

Surprisingly, Carla didn't seem greatly upset, but instead remained hopeful.

"She really took out after me when I walked in the place all dressed up and all. But she don't know how fine it can be, how right I feel just bein' in that place. I know I gotta get back there, Sister Davis. I have faith, something's gotta happen, you know? Somethin's gotta happen."

And that was the phrase we echoed over and over in our minds and hearts that week as we two worried missionaries went about our business of calling upon the faithful and unfaithful alike. How many times over breakfast did DiNate's ebony eyes fill? How often as we trudged along country roads did that very phrase escape my lips to lay upon the changing winds like a prayer, even then an epithet? In the quiet of our bedroom at night, after the last prayers were uttered and the final amens posted upon the billboards of heaven did we both lie there waiting for blessed sleep and utter to the noiseless room one more time

"Something's gotta happen. Lord?"

But nothing changed that week or the next. Phone calls from the battle site, the "lake front" we called it, dwindled. To make matters more intense it was leaked to us that we were candidates to be transferred the following month to a small ward twenty or so miles to the north to replace two young sisters who were needed closer to mission headquarters. Our "good news" was not accompanied by any particular species of fowl, but indeed relayed early on a Sabbath morning by our zone leader via the trusty telephone.

"Oh, dear me, that's what I feared," DiNate moaned, getting back in bed and pulling her pillow over her face. She carried on a lengthy, emotional conversation with it in Italian and then wiped her eyes with the blanket.

Too worried to cry, I escaped to the bathroom. The shower rained tears upon me that morning and I applied eye makeup over puffy lids that kept wetting themselves. This is no way to start a day, I told my face in the mirror. Something's gotta happen."

We fired up Bambina with heavy hearts and started our day's journey to visit some members who had fallen away. The skies were cloudy but summer air hung heavy and wet against the trees and we sensed another steamer of a day. The perfectly aligned white fences that had seemed to me just a few months past to be the trim of a crown upon the grassy hills now became barriers to the progress of the spirit. Maybe Texas was no different than any other unwelcoming place and those hapless few who traversed her in the name of the Lord were by and large destined for rejection and failure. Never underestimate the power of the Adversary, I told DiNate in somber tones. That old traitor's fighting hard for Carla.

Sister DiNate shook her head philosophically.

"We got to think of something, we make that woman change her mind."

"It's a change of heart that's needed. Only the Lord can bring that."

We drove along in silence, listening to Bambina's steady hum. A squirrel darted across the highway just ahead. Then a new impulse came to me with sudden force.

"Stop here, right here."

"What? You want I stop middle of the road?"

"Yes. Right now. We've gotta ask again, but with real hope, don't you see? Pull over, pull over in that field up ahead."

DiNate looked at me in wonder, but obeyed. Bambina came to a screeching halt on the grassy shoulder of the two-lane country road. Hurriedly we disembarked and climbed unsteadily over mounds of earth covered with gay bluebonnets and brilliant Indian paintbrush. There we found a somewhat secluded bower beneath a couple of scrub pines sufficiently hidden from the road.

"Kneel," I commanded us, but my companion was already falling to her knees in the dirt. For what seemed like hours that followed we were as obsessed women, passionately engaged in prayer before the Bar of the Universe, seeking out our Heavenly Father, beseeching Him to give us instruction, to bestow upon Carla His peace, to soften Mrs. Sloan's angry heart, offering Him our lives if necessary if He would let us bring Carla's golden spirit into the waters of baptism before we left the area, that she could claim that most precious possession; a cleansed, obedient and God-loving soul.

So engrossed were we in our plaints that our cries became a dialogue between us and we spoke from two mouths but were in that defining hour of only one mind. Hands met and held in a vise of determined effort. Two hearts knelt in prayer; one arose in Christ. My companion and I can testify that many more were with us unseen in that bower that afternoon . . .

When we'd said the last amen we cried and hugged and wiped away each other's tears. We felt so much lighter! I picked a fragrant bouquet of bluebonnets for those we were yet to meet. It had become a truly lovely summer Texas day and for once we didn't at all mind the heat and swelter then, for we were amidst carpets of wildflowers whipped by southern breezes, serenaded by cardinals and mockingbird phrases and awed by flocks of Canada geese flying noisily north.

"Let go and let God take over," I remembered from long ago when that heavenly sight appeared to me in the Missouri grove. Sister DiNate broke forth in a suddenly remembered fragment from Rigoletto and we commenced our day's journey with renewed hope and vigor.

Brother Tiger, always prompt and concerned for the welfare of his animals, called us early on our P-day while we gathered our wash and prepared to clean our cluttered apartment. The phone rang five times before I got to it.

"Oh, you're there, good! My oldest, Jasper? He's not eating right. Just picks at the grass. I had to take his mate to the vet and I think he's mourning for her. Delilah Parrey and I are going to that feed store by the lake to get their special feed. Her horses love it, you know. We thought the llamas might go for it. Wondered if you two'd like to come along?"

"We're on our P-day, Brother Tiger. Trying to get our own house in order. But thanks for thinking of us. We'll see you tomorrow in church."

"Yeah, well, we have someone for you to meet, actually . . . I know you're on your day off and all, but this is kind of a special thing . . . We'd really like you to come with us. It will just take about an hour."

Brother Tiger was nothing if not sincere and he sounded like it was urgently important to us. I think he was forcing himself to be casual. Something told me to consider it. I told him I'd ask Sister DiNate. She looked at me like I'd just offered to do her laundry for six months. "Si`, si`, e`bella. Marvelous! I take it, I go. Washing will wait, let's go."

"We'll swing by at noon. See you then," he said happily and the phone clicked off.

A couple of hours later we had donned dresses and lipstick and were on the long hot highway that meandered through the hills to the lake roads. DiNate and I were securely fastened in the back seat of Sister Parrey's new green and gold decorator van. From the CD player the "surround sound" of Hank Williams Sr. cried in our ears while fatted white and red-umber Angus strolled the summer hillsides, munching grass and dandelions. It was a coolish day, a bit cloudy toward the east and north. DiNate was singing along with Hank, trying mightily to paste a Texas accent over her Italian. Sister Parrey laughed so hard her van nearly hit a ditch. I was relaxed and beginning to feel deliciously drowsy. Then Sister Parrey turned off the highway onto a sand stubbled farm road that led to the lake. Suddenly I remembered traveling down the same road. It didn't lead to any businesses, but instead into a mobile home park.

"This looks like —." Isn't this where Carla —?"

But my words died in my mouth. The van turned onto an unpaved street. Brambles climbed along the shoulders of the packed dirt road like natural barbed wire. Scrub pines obscured the light ahead. It was Carla's street.

DiNate said something under her breath. Ahead of us Mrs. Sloan's trailer sagged like a sick white whale, deep in tall grass, rotting boards piled around it. Shades were drawn, there was no sign of life. It was like a coffin with a door and windows. I wondered how anyone could live in that rusty old can and call it home.

The van passed Carla's house and stopped two houses down. Norman Tiger opened his door and then held ours open. Sister Parrey was already out of the driver's seat and heading toward an old Chevy pickup parked further down the street.

"What's going on, Norman?" I asked. "You told us we were going to a feed store. What are we doing here, has Carla called for us or — ?"

But Norman just stammered his apology and in a worried, hesitant way he shrugged and motioned for us to follow him.

"Please, trust me again, honest, you'll see why in a minute."

DiNate and I looked at each other, completely mystified. She let a low whistle escape her lips and adjusted her silver hair clip. Silently, we turned and followed Brother Tiger.

A few seconds later another pickup appeared and several more cars trailed behind it in caravan. Norman waved to the driver of the lead car as it passed us. It was the Werners.

"What the —?" DiNate spread her arms in a huge question.

Brother Tiger turned around. He was grinning broadly now that others had arrived.

"Sisters, if you'll forgive me for my little lie today, — he raised his arm toward the other vehicles — we all want to be a part of the missionary work you're doing here. Would you like that?"

Before we could answer, Sister Parrey reappeared ahead of us, her arms around several youngsters. Other children were skipping along behind her. We recognized the youth that she drove to Dallas for proxy baptisms. Every child wore a suit and tie. They crossed the road and gaily joined the other arrivals who were convening at a spot several houses down from Carla's. The street had come alive with church members! Everyone was smiling like a party was about to start. Now more trucks were pulling around the corner, quietly parking along the street. When I finally regained my senses I counted twenty five branch members including children and a dozen cars and trucks. Everyone was wearing go-to-meeting clothes. It was Monday, not yet noon.

"This cannot be, it's not Sunday! Why everybody dressed up?"

DiNate wanted to know. We stared at the sight around us, dumb as ducks. Then Brother Tiger motioned us to the Werners' truck, telling us to wait there. From inside the truck he brought out two camp chairs for us to sit on, then hurried away again to another meeting that was apparently taking place down the road. As we watched, they all gathered in a circle and bowed their heads in prayer.

In a few minutes everyone dispersed again to their vehicles and as we watched in amazement they came forth carrying boxes. Even the children carried objects. As they got closer we saw the boxes were labelled on the outside.

"Oh, my gosh," I said. "They're carrying food storage! They're taking those boxes to Carla's house!"

Sure enough, the brethren and the women, too carried food storage and clothes, tools and packages of planting soil. Silently they made an informal line and quietly beside the broken concrete steps outside Mrs. Sloan's trailer, they piled the boxes one upon another just to the side of the path, making sure each box showed its label of contents. It looked like a pilgrimage! More than a fourth of the active branch was represented, and half again as many children, but they moved with such unity and coordination of effort that I felt they must have rehearsed, for it seemed they performed in perfect unison.

No one inside the trailer responded, yet if someone were home they surely would have heard the rustling and piling of boxes going on just outside that old wooden door. But none of the dedicated workers stopped to contemplate or to knock. Like solemn soldiers, everyone quietly attended to duty. Not even the children spoke. Within about 30 minutes there were sixteen stacks of boxes, clothes, seed and soil bestowed upon the "lawn" outside the Sloan trailer. I turned to my companion. Tears made it hard to speak.

"This is one you can tell your grandchildren, Sister. This wasn't in our lessons, you know?"

"I can't believe — I never think that this. Mama mia, we witness a miracle here, yes?"

"Any miracle will have to happen inside that scarred-up old metal can . . . "

Having finished their loading and carrying, the people gathered at the dirt curb in front of Carla's place. The children were off to the side with Sister Parrey. Then Sister Kenmore, the just-released choir director, stepped forward and began to sing "I Believe in Christ" in her sweet, high soprano. Her arm rose and fell in rhythm and everyone joined her softly and with real feeling. My companion and I joined in. It was a moment that united us in an outpouring of love.

And slowly the rotting old door opened. A small, bony figure of a woman stood like a defending soldier in her doorway, arms across her breast, shoulders hunched in anger. The group, if they saw her, continued to sing. Mrs. Sloan stood for a long moment, as though letting her anger grow and flush inside her. Suddenly, I saw a glint of blue steel flash in the sun that filtered through the scrub pines. A heavy object was raised slowly but surely to the old woman's waist, barrel pointing to the steps below. My reaction came in a near shout. I grabbed DiNate.

"Oh, no! She's got a rifle!"

"Dio mio!"

Everyone heard us. They stopped singing and turned to look, but not one turned to leave. We were all frozen to the spot.

The cracked, hard voice shot words like bullets from the doorway.

"This here rifle's loaded, just so's you know, and I ain't afraid to use it. Now I don't want you here, any of you, so git off my land now!"

No one moved. I don't know why. In my heart, I really felt she'd shoot at us if we didn't leave. Maybe this was one fight we weren't going to win.

Then Jimmy Frank stepped out of the crowd of children and started walking toward the trailer. He was the oldest boy, a child of record, baptized two years ago. Not a particularly noticeable child, he seemed to like adult company and had come along primarily for the ride, his mother told me later.

"Jimmy, don't!" Sister Werner yelled. Delilah Parrey growled "James Frank, you get back here," but he continued slowly forward as if he hadn't heard, directly in the path of the rifle. In his hand was a greeting card.

Then Morgan moved forward. She always followed Jimmy wherever he'd let her, but he didn't turn around. Then Janine Falk and the Wolfs' boy. Mrs. Sloan didn't seem to blink, instead she shouted even louder and that rifle lay in her arms like insurance.

"Hey. You heard me, now back up and git outta here! I ain't afraid to shoot."

"Oh, God," Sister DiNate moaned quietly, dropping to her knees in the grass. "Dear Father, this woman, she full of anger. Soften her heart, let her reach out. These children, they must live. Please, give your miracle now."

I went to her as she dedicated her prayer and we held tightly to each other.

More children were walking toward Mrs. Sloan. The adults came to life and hurried forth to retrieve them, adding their bodies to the potential line of direct fire, but they didn't seem afraid. It all happened with such surprise and suddenness that none of the members attempted to deal with this distraught woman's threats or the business end of her Winchester. Their only concern was to protect the children.

Then a funny thing happened. Jimmy Frank had almost reached the trailer. Showing no fear he stopped and opened his card. He began to read out loud. It was addressed to "Carla's grandmother" and it said that he, Jimmy Frank, loved Carla and wanted to be her friend and that he'd like to know "gramma", too. Jimmy's parents reached him. They stood with him.

Janine also had been given a card. She opened hers and started reading it louder than Jimmy had. It said the same thing. Unknown to DiNate and myself, all the children had been given cards, Sister Parrey's idea, and they were supposed to leave them on the front porch "where that mean woman can't miss them, you know? Then she'll read them and that will soften her up some. It's better than doing nothing, isn't it?"

But one by one each child walked up to stand behind Jimmy, and one by one they absorbed themselves in opening the little pink gummy envelopes and digging out the contents. Then dutifully they each read the words over and over again, a busy chorus of little voices. Parents gathered protectively around them.

"We love you, Carla. We are so happy you came to our church. Will you come again so we can be your friends? And please bring your very nice gramma."

It was a moment out of the macabre. I'm grateful now that those sweet spirits never realized the "very nice gramma" they sang about so naively was only 25 feet from them holding a "squirrel gun" to her face like a hunter waiting for his game to arrive.

Then slowly and, it seemed, with great reluctance, she lowered her weapon, but her face was stone. Mrs. Sloan looked at the boxes of food and seed around her. Her eyes rested on the pile of clothes and planting soil. Then she looked at all of us all over her yard, the way we were holding onto the children and each other. No one spoke or seemed to know what to do next. DiNate and I exchanged looks. Should we be the ones? After all, we were the missionaries, but that rifle now rested against the door jamb. I held my breath. Slowly we moved toward her to assure her we meant no harm (and then we'd all get out of there as fast as we could!).

Pop! The ear-tearing sound of an engine on a rampage, banging and steaming its way up the street, changed everything. An ugly pink and black pickup roared toward us. It careened around the other cars on the street and screeched to a dusty stop at the dirt curb in front of the trailer, forcing us to make a quick dash for Parrey's van. Benny G, hair glossed and raised above his pate, bounced out the door smiling wide, sucking on a barber pole colored straw that disappeared into a cup of frothy root beer. Carla disembarked from the other side, Benny's leather and metal-studded jacket hanging on her shoulders. It was 1:45. He was bringing her home from school.

It was quite a picture Carla took in as she stepped gaily out of Benny G's truck. Instantly her expression changed to one of shock as she saw her grandmother facing off the branch members and children on the lawn. She threw off the jacket and walked quickly toward the trailer, putting her own body between the woman and everyone else. Mrs. Sloan turned and quickly put her rifle out of sight behind the door.

"Granmamau, what are you doing? What's going on?"

Mrs. Sloan, seeing Benny G with Carla, quickly switched her attention.

"Carla, come in here and get away from that stupid boy. I've told you not to see him again."

But Carla was not being intimidated. Stopped solid before her grandmother she stood with hands on hips. She tossed her red hair in defiance and spoke in a steel firm voice.

"Granmamau, these people are my friends. I didn't know they were coming but they're welcome here. If you're mean to any one of them then you gotta answer to God, and I ain't obeying you no more, you hear, and we both know I'm all you got left. Now, are you gonna respect what I want or not?"

The old woman wavered. Her eyes studied the dirt, her mouth a line of iron. There was silence while she contemplated her moves. It was plain that Carla's words had found their target like a magnet, but how much effect would they have?

❧

The small congregation on the lawn had fallen to talking quietly among themselves. They still gave no signs of leaving. Sister Parrey was in her van with her head bowed. We knew it wasn't over yet.

The old woman raised her head and in her tired eyes there were now tears instead of fire. Her arms opened up slowly to reach for Carla, who came into them, and the two held each other a long moment. Suddenly the woman seemed short and frail as she leaned heavily upon the strong young girl who held her. I think I heard Mrs. Sloan say

"Honey, I'm trying to keep you safe. I'm sorry," but I couldn't be sure.

Carla, who loved to forgive, kissed her grandmother's neck and spoke quietly to her. I was amazed to see the old woman start to shake. In a moment she pulled away and wiped her eyes on her sleeve. On Carla's face, half-turned toward us, we saw a gentle smile begin.

"Gee, that's great," Benny G said, draining the last of his soda. "I got kinda worried there for a minute, know what I mean?"

We knew. I think everyone breathed relief in that second as we witnessed the power of love, great and unseen, that was really in charge of this meeting.

Brother Tiger said loudly

"Well, these ladies probably have a lot to talk over, folks. Maybe we all ought be on our way." There were murmurs of agreement and everyone turned to leave.

"Wait, please."

Carla and her grandmother, arms around each other, stepped off the porch and came into our midst. All traces of anger seemed to have left Mrs. Sloan. She stood sheepishly, almost not raising her eyes. Jimmy Frank was in front of her. He reached out his thank you card and handed it to her. Then the other children came over and gave her their cards.

"We love you, old gramma," he said. "Do you have any cookies?"

Things were moving too fast for Mrs. Sloan, so Carla spoke up.

"Granmamau and I are grateful to you all for your food and the things you brought us. She says it'll be all right if I go to church with you all, too. She's just not used to good folks no more, ain't that so?"

Mrs. Sloan looked at DiNate. Then she looked at Jimmy Franks and Brother Werner and shook her gray head slowly.

"I reckon I forgot my manners with you all . . . know you mean no harm. That food and seed, I ain't got none of that. Now we kin have a small harvest here, been a long time since anythin' good's grown here.

Carla nudged her grandmother's shoulder. Plainly, the woman was fighting within herself now, but the stakes were too high to ignore.

"Well . . . I allow . . . look here, now . . . Carla says she wants to join this here church . . . I was brought up Mormon but I ain't no belonger to no church." She tossed her head with pride. She hesitated, still reticent to give up what she'd been holding back all those years.

"Carla's always been safe with me," she began. I protect her good."

Then Carla turned to look her grandmother in the eyes and with perfect sense and timing she answered back

"Yes, ma'am, but I am far safer with Christ."

"Amen to that," said Brother Tiger softly. A softer chorus of "amens" followed his.

Mrs. Sloan paused, I think she knew she'd been bettered.

"Well, we'll see," she said, managing a tight smile. "I got a reputation here for being fair, so we'll just see. I got legal custody, you just remember that when you try and baptize her with no permission."

We assured Mrs. Sloan that her wishes would be respected, but Carla was already smiling as if she could see herself at the font.

"Hey," demanded little Jimmy Franks, who'd been impatiently waiting for an answer while we worked things out. "You got any cookies in there or not?"

ॐ

Benny G had stopped near DiNate, who barely looked at him. He gave her a wink. Then, unaccountably, she sucked in her breath and squealed "Oh" so loudly that many turned to see what was wrong. She pointed to the necklace around Benny G's throat. It was a chain of links, made of heavy silver and I guessed it to be another part of the rapper culture, but at it's center, dangling just above his open shirt button, was a sleek silver charm not much larger than a thumb. It was a bird in flight, wings outspread across his clavicle and beak pointed ahead toward some unknown, fixed destination. I remembered her remark earlier about God sending a bird as messenger as a sign of spiritual awakening. I gave DiNate a hard stare and shook a finger at her.

"That's pushing it, Sister."

She shrugged in that singularly Italian way and returned an impish grin. "Just teasing, mi amica."

It took more time, but we did see Carla baptized and given the gift of the Holy Ghost, though she couldn't get her grandmother to attend the ceremony. Mrs. Sloan did give Carla money for several new dresses to wear to church. Benny G was there sans leather jacket, cheering her on. His mother forced him to wear a suit jacket and tie and eagerly came with him to witness Carla's grand moment in the waters of life.

Jimmy Franks finally agreed to wear his hearing aid. He'd been too worried about the other kids taunting him to put it on that day at Mrs. Sloan's. I didn't even know he was legally deaf and was learning sign language until his father told me. Then I realized why he hadn't responded to Sister Parray or his parents' calling to him when he stepped fearlessly in front of Carla's grandmother.

Sister DiNate and I were transferred up the road to Fairview a month later, where we found other souls meet for the love of God and willing to prove it in the way we love best. Sister Parray threw us a surprise barbecue before we left — with beans, ribs and lots of fried potatoes, so DiNate didn't have time to go on a fast. After the meal she led everyone in the reprise from Barber of Seville.

But, looking back, a fond memory of that indelible time is of my friend the Italian balaboosta, a stout-hearted warrior for the Lord fresh from the marble pits of Barre as she stands barefoot in a meadow deep in south central Texas, her feet spread, arms raised with abandon before hovering trees gently swaying in the heat. In each hand she holds a shoe, and there before a summer audience that boasts a forest aviary she throws back her head. From her cultured throat pours with gusto and like thick sauce the triumphant Serenade from the opera Don Giovanni, in which the heroine sings of love's sweetness lost and rediscovered, and of renewed hope, her hearty prayer of praise for new beginnings.

THE END

Anythingspossible Penguin —

At the bottom of our world where icicles grow all year 'round there is a group of islands shaped like birds in flight called the Penguinese Islands. These small particles of land, the true ancestral home of all the world's penguins, are always covered by snow. They look like huge ice cones as they seem to float upon the sea. The most famous of all these small, bird shaped islands is called Bird Rock.

If you sail past Bird Rock in an iceboat you may see these gentle birds, all dressed up in their best tuxedo and tails outfits, sunning high upon the glaciers, then sliding into the freezing Antarctic waters for a midmorning dip or a lazy afternoon swim.

Penguins always wear black and white and look as though they have just put on very comfortable pajamas. They are short-haired and sleek, with beaks thin and pointed, more like pens than hooks. They always stand at attention in a very serious way. Penguins walk somewhat as we do, but there is webbing between their toes, so they seem to move from side to side as they walk straight ahead. Heavenly Father was so pleased with these polite, upstanding birds that He gave them flippers instead of wings, so they would not fall over as they walk. They can swim fast and dive deep to catch fish. They can also move very fast in the frozen waters where they frolic much of the time.

There is a legend about the most famous penguin on Bird Rock who was called Number One on Monday. He was so named because he was the first penguin baby born to his family on that Monday. It was customary then as now to number offspring in the order of birth, so parent penguins can know who is who.

Number One on Monday was a very independent son. He was also an excellent student in class and earned many special fish tidbit awards from his teachers. He was special, too, because he believed he would one day be able to fly. In this way Number One on Monday was unique because penguins, it is safe to say, have never flown anywhere! So this little penguin's dream of flight seemed just wishful thinking. But to him it was almost real. When he stood before the ice mirror each morning he imagined himself soaring high above the islands, and this dream gave him much happiness.

His mother had complete faith in her son. She made him a warm mackinaw and a bright flight cap from material washed up on the shore. His father was proud of his first son and taught him much about wind and air currents. His brothers and sisters always encouraged him and said they hoped he would succeed, but Number One on Monday knew in his heart of hearts that everyone was just being kind, because every bird on Bird Rock knew it was not possible for a penguin to fly.

One day Number One on Monday said to himself: "To be a special penguin I must have a special name, for when I do learn how to fly I will be famous all over the Penguinese Islands."

He spent many hours deep in thought in his favorite position: resting on his heels while leaning back on his flippers. Sometimes he thought so hard he forgot he was leaning and fell over. His friend, Third Bird, observed him and said

"You are not like the rest of us. We all know that penguins were not meant to fly like the seagulls. Do you really think you can do what we cannot?"

"Anything is possible," Number One on Monday replied loudly and with great certainty. Suddenly he stopped and thought a minute. "That's the perfect name for me! Anythingspossible Penguin! One day I shall fly to all the islands of the Penguinese! He ran home to tell his parents of his new name.

Thereafter, Anythingspossible Penguin tried very hard to learn to soar into the skies over Bird Rock. His friends watched him but did not know what to think.

"He's gone crazy from too much sun," said One of the Few.

"He will soon stop this nonsense when he falls flat on his beak a few times," sniffed Six On Thursday Past as they watched. Anythingspossible Penguin slide and skid down the icy slopes nearby.

"If birds could fly, fish could talk," said another. "Just what does he think he is?"

Penguins believe in holding lots of meetings, and they always listen to each other's opinions. It was the common consensus among their leaders that what has always been shall always be. They did not approve, therefore, of this young upstart's rebellious ideas. They all voted to ignore his attempts at flying and strongly urged each other to be content with the status quo.

But Anythingspossible Penguin paid no attention. He knew he was different but he believed that his dream of flight could somehow come true. Then he would show the others how to make their own lives more fun.

As he grew older his determination grew. He never tired of seeking new ways to lift himself off the ice, though it was difficult because penguins are heavy and fat so they can keep very warm in the freezing weather. At first he tried to fly straight up out of the water. Dressed in the flight cap and mackinaw, he dived off his favorite rock into the icy ocean below. He pedaled his webbed feet as quickly as he could and moved his strong flippers around and around. Soon the water was twisting and churning. But the stubborn little penguin kept flapping and flapping. From the rocks above he could hear the other birds laughing at him. He tried not to notice them.

"I will find a way or my name is not Tout est possible penguine" he said in perfect French, which he was learning from reading French magazines that washed up on the beaches of Bird Rock from French-speaking countries.

The very next day Anythingspossible Penguin was up early and out on the iceberg whistling a happy tune. Tied onto his webbed feet were long black rubber sleds made up of old tires he found washed up on the island. He waddled and sloshed until he came to the top of a hill. The wind was cold at his back. That is good, he thought, for it will give me extra speed. Raising his flat feet into the air he gave a loud "Honk" and pushed himself off down the hill. How exciting it was!

He went faster and faster! Down the icy slopes he raced, his eyes on the place where his wings would take him aloft. Suddenly it was time to jump. "Here I go," he shouted, pumping his flippers up and down as fast as they would move. He gathered his short legs beneath him and jumped off the slope. His little round body shot into the air like a slick bullet.

Whomp! Splat!

"Look out!" He smacked head first into a snowbank. "Oh, dear" he groaned into the snow. His beak was stuck in the ice. "This is not the way to fly," he said, spitting out the ice. Behind him were the other penguins. Third Bird couldn't contain himself. He fell over and rolled around with laughter. Six on Thursday Past just sat sadly and shook his black beak from side to side.

"Right," he said. "Perfect."

Our hero was very embarrassed. Head hanging, he hobbled off, mumbling to himself in Spanish,

"Todo es posible" to keep his spirits up, but he was a very sad penguin.

If AnythingspossiblePenguin had been an average bird he would have sat back on his flippers and never again even thought of flying. But he knew a secret from a book that had long ago washed upon the shores of Bird Rock. He had learned a great deal about the world from the wonderful things that came to Bird Rock beach on the daily tides. None of the other birds seemed interested in finding these treasures from other lands.

This book was slim and very wet but it contained pictures of stars. There were even samples of wishes that could be made when the stars came out at night. The book said that a Great Creator of all things was in charge of the nighttime sky and that He personally ordered all the stars to shine forth each night from their special places to give hope and promise to all on the earth. Our courageous penguin looked now for the section on flying.

The instructions said that he must offer thanks to the Great Creator for all he had been given, including his wish to fly, and then to ask for help in working out his problem. Then he must sleep beneath the stars and dream his dearest dream, believing that he would be blessed with an answer to his quest. The book also said that the Great Creator often granted wishes through His heavenly helpers on the condition that the one asking favors would be helpful to others if his dream came true.

The next night, Anythingspossible Penguin, wearing his gaily colored flight cap and green mackinaw, journeyed to his favorite thinking and praying place to spend the night beneath the stars again, his book beneath his flipper and courage welling in his breast. There he spoke to the Great Creator and asked for the ability to fly to all the islands of the Penguinese, promising his help to any other penguin that asked him. Then he slept deeply and had wonderful dreams in which he led hundreds of his fellow penguins in a long line around their island home.

Next morning the citizens of Bird Rock beheld a curious sight as they waddled outside their icegloos for a stroll. There sat Any thingspossible Penguin on an icy rock above them. His flippers were stretched at his sides, his eyes closed. On his head, like a crown, sat the flight cap. His green woolen mackinaw was slung around his throat, making a colorful contrast on his snowy white chest. He was still as a statue.

"Omigosh," said Third Bird. "He's frozen to death!"

"That's not possible," corrected Six on Thursday Past, opening and closing his beak with sarcasm. "More likely, he's asleep. Ha, ha! What a silly whiz he is."

"Shall we go help him?" asked little Last One, hopefully wagging her tail feathers.

"Yes," they all shouted in unison, waddling over to see what was the matter with their friend. They gathered around him and cooed, but Any-thingspossible Penguin did not notice, for he was deep in concentration.

"I want to fly. I must fly. I will fly," they heard him mumble over and over again. Then he said loudly "It's all in how you think about it!" And then he said "Tutto e possible, tudo possivel est" in Italian and Portuguese.

Hearing this the penguins were amazed that their friend knew other languages. "How talented he is," they said in wonder and amazement. "How very clever and learned." And they all wished they could understand the strange and beautiful things their friend was saying, for they had never heard these words before.

But Anythingspossible Penguin paid them no heed. Any moment now, he thought, I shall awaken to find myself soaring through the skies, sailing upon the currents of air and then beak-diving for fish. He could even taste those fish. They would almost jump into his mouth!

Ever so slowly, he began moving his flippers up and down. His short tail kept time behind him, making him rock back and forth. His friends were startled. They backed away. Suddenly our hero jumped straight into the air!

Uh, oh. SLAM! Back onto the ice he fell, bottom first. His flight cap rolled off his head and landed in a puddle. His green scarf was tangled between his legs.

"Omigosh", he groaned "This is not the way to fly. This is not going to work." And even though he was a very proud penguin he buried his head in his flippers and cried and cried.

Soon he heard noises all around him. Looking up he saw his friends gathered around, smiling down at him.

"I guess I really can't fly," he wailed.

"Perhaps not," said One Of The Few, who had known Anythingspossible Penguin when he was still Number One on Monday. "Maybe you aren't any different than the rest of us when it comes to flying, but you can sure speak better. Where have you learned all those languages? How many do you know? Will you teach them to us?"

Then all the other penguins took up the cry.

"Oh, yes. Please teach us how to speak in those foreign tongues," cried Third Bird.

"Fine, just fine." said Six on Thursday Past. "That's all we need, our own United Nations."

"Charming, I'm sure," giggled little Last One.

7 Now Anythingspossible Penguin sat up in amazement. He was very surprised and disappointed to learn that no one else seemed to really care if he could fly or not! They only wanted to know how to speak the many languages he had learned from his travels along the Bird Rock coastline.

Now Anythingspossible Penguin rose to his full height. He walked thoughtfully up and down the ice, talking and thinking to himself. By now he was realizing that he could not make himself fly. He wanted to do that so very much, but he knew that teaching his friends to speak in many languages would give them great pleasure. He loved his friends dearly. Maybe he could help them to achieve great things during their lives on Bird Rock. He thought of the prayers he had made to the Great Creator and remembered his promise to be helpful to others.

"Can it be true," he asked them finally, "that penguins are really not made to fly?"

"Don't know how we'd manage it," Third Bird pointed out. "Besides, none of us want to fly."

"Right-o, good buddy," intoned Six on Thursday Past, "we're fishers, not fliers."

Last One moved close to our befuddled hero and tenderly put her flipper into his. "I think you can do anything you put your mind to," she said sweetly. "But perhaps there is more than one way to get this project off the ground." She was a smart bird, though very young.

"I can tell you that if we all put our heads together, in as short a time as penguins can take, maybe we can figure this out."

Anythingspossible Penguin listened intently. He was amazed and very happy at the loyalty and hope his friends expressed. But, though he had lived all his life on this island he had never asked a favor of anyone. He felt that his dream of flying was his problem and that he had no right to ask for help. He walked around the island thinking and muttering. Then he had an idea.

I will go to Heavenly Father, he thought. The Great Creator will know what I should do.

Happy that he had finally found a way to have his problems answered, Anythingspossible Penguin immediately crossed his flippers and began to pray. He prayed all that night and then fell asleep, far from his icegloo. The stars in Heaven winked at him while he slept, and sang lullabies in many languages.

The next day was clear and warm, as warm as frigid weather can be. Our little hero awoke with hope in his heart and a new way of seeing things. Excitedly, he rushed off to find his friends. They were smart, too. Six On Thursday Past could build ice-gloos in a day if a mean storm was on its way. Another pal could make skis. Third Bird was a master ice slider and One Of The Few claimed to see far into the future. Little One was a talented seamstress.

"Okay, fellas," he said, feeling happier with every word. "Let's put our talents together. I'll teach you how to say "ANYTHING IS POSSIBLE!" in many wonderful languages and together we can figure out a way to fly."

"Marvelous," the others cheered. Even Six On Thursday Past was happy. "Let's all get to work!" They were overjoyed at the prospect ahead, so they celebrated with a big party and served their favorite imitation seal punch and snowfish cookies.

For the next few months Anythingspossible Penguin and his friends were a busy crew, learning to say "ANYTHING IS POSSIBLE" first in all the romance languages (because they were truly romantic), then in Greek (because it was Greek to them), and finally they learned the mysterious tongues of the Orient (because they were a mystery). They could be seen skiing down slopes over and over again, jumping off icy ledges wearing new sealskin beanies with twirlers on top, practicing levitation on mountaintops, testing wind currents with their beaks, or just quietly staring into space, deep in thought. But the answers were very slow in coming.

Then one day it happened. Anythingspossible Penguin took all their best ideas and put them together into one workable idea. He thought about his dreams and how he had imagined himself flying through the air. He closed his eyes and imagined himself in flight. There it was! It all came together! He knew suddenly just how to do it! Everyone had contributed their best ideas. They had truly invented an engineering marvel there at the bottom of the world. It was the first of its kind — the marvelous Penguiplane!

It had a smart beanie cap with a rotor on top that whirled in the wind The wings were like a gull's but made of seal, heavy enough for a penguin's long, rounded body. Another rotor was wound around the penguin's tail feathers for balance. A pair of extra slick sealskin skis for the pushoffs from the ice completed the outfit. Atop the rotors of this marvelous Penguiplane were streamers of many colors floating gaily in the wind.

When all the parts were put together, Anythingspossible Penguin put them on and climbed to the top of the island's highest iceberg. His new outfit was really not heavy at all, and felt quite sturdy. Then he said a prayer, gathered his courage and leapt from the ice into the sky!

Ohmigosh! Hold your breath! He flew! The rotors caught the wind and breezes from the recent storms kept his sealskin wings buoyant. The currents caught him and he rose above the icecap and actually sailed on the air! He found that wagging his little tail feathers helped, too. Putting it all together, flapping his flippers and bobbing his head up and down to catch the breeze in the rotor atop his cap, Anythingspossible Penguin soared all around the island, not too high, not too low, but just right.

On the ground, his friends cheered.

"He's done it," said Third Bird. "Would you look at that!"

"Fine," droned Six On Thursday Past. Next thing you know, we'll have a Penguiport on Bird Rock, smog and a sky full of flying penguins." But he really was happy for his friend.

"I think he's so handsome," signed Little One. "Maybe we can fly together some day?"

All the other penguins on all of the Penguinese Islands looked up from their morning meetings and saw the strangest sight: they saw a penguin, just like themselves, wearing a cap with a whirling rotor turning in the wind and long sealskin flappers around his body. Another rotor held up his tail!

"What is that?" they all asked in unison. "It cannot be a penguin, because penguins do not fly. Perhaps it is a new kind of bird."

They laughed, feeling very wise, indeed, then returned to their meetings.

And so, Anythingspossible Penguin realized his dream of flight with lots of hard work, lots of help from his friends, and lots of blessings from the Great Creator. Soon they were all in great demand as teachers of many languages to other penguins on all the islands of the Penguinese. They first taught every penguin to say "ANYTHING IS POSSIBLE" in numerous languages. The level of language ability in the Penguinese increased so much that a university was erected upon Bird Island in honor of world-wide literacy and understanding. And that is why the penguins of the world can today communicate easily with anyone. If you listen carefully you can hear them. Here is just a smattering of the languages they speak.

In Arabic: *Kull mumkin!*

In Vietnamese: *Cat gi cung co the xay ra!*

In Korean: *Muo-si-dun-ji itda kanung-han!*

In German: *Alles ist maglich!*

In Latin: *Quid fieri potest!*

In Hebrew: *Fshar oseh kol ad varim*

And in Pig Latin: *Anything's ay ossible pay!*

Here is a rare old picture of this famous fellow in his Penguiplane, flight cap and green mackinaw, soaring and coasting, racing and diving in the cold crystal skies above his dear home on Bird Rock.

Now, dear Reader: How can you make your dreams come true?

BIRD ROCK

DRAWN BY A FRIEND

SHEET MUSIC

A Song To Be Sung —

Into His Rest
Moroni 7:3

Words by Gabriele Titze Burgess
Marlena Tanya Muchnick

Gabriele Titze Burgess

A Song To Be Sung, 2 —

Into His Rest

In - to His rest _____ freed from all doubt, _____ heart o - pen

now _____ from side out. _____ In - to His rest, no-thing to

hide, I come to Him _____ arms o - pen wide.

A Song To Be Sung, 3 —

Long have I fal-tered so full of doubt, ____ al - low-ing pri - de to

lock me out. ____ But pray-er up-on that sac - red name ____

a-wakes my heart con sumes all shame. In-to His rest, freed from all

A Song To Be Sung, 4 —

Into His Rest

doubt, heart o - pen now _____ from in - side out. In - to His

rest _____ no - thing to hide, I come to Him _____ arms o - pen

wide. I kneel re - pen - tant my life's re - stored, _____

A Song To Be Sung, 5 —

mer-ci-ful Sa-vior, my pain's no more.___ Thy he-aling ba-lm of

peace sub-lime ___ thy glo-rious love tran-scends all time. In-to His

rest, freed from all doubt, Heart o-pen now from in-side

6

Into His Rest

A Psalm to Be Spoken, 1 —

Song of the Christ
A Spoken Psalm

Words by Marlena Tanya Muchnick
Music by Gabriele Titze Burgess

A Psalm to Be Spoken, 2 —

Song of the Christ

live at thy behest. Thou ministers and proves our best; thou knows our

lives, our faith, our home above. _____ Thou wast sent by He

who..formed thee..in..the belly of a maid. She birthed thee..in..that..humble

room..unlike..the heavenly womb where death and sin dwell not, nor price..be..paid. Thou

came and died amongst our kind.. .but..from..that tomb,..thy..cave..of..stone.

A Psalm to Be Spoken, 3 —

Thou rose and took thy life again then walked..among..the sons..of..men.

That..we might live new seeds..of..life.. were sown. Oh,..sower

of..eternal..lives let us prepare..a..path for..thee of spirits who will serve their Christ; a bridge

of..love and..sacrifice; meet..for thy innocense and purity. Give us this day thy bread of life.

A Psalm to Be Spoken, 4 —

Song of the Christ

The..sacrament   of   broken crust   that..it..may   lead   us   to   our   Feast

of   endless..life,   that   e'en   the   least..can   know..his..king   who   reigns   among   the   just.   Oh,

help..me   now,..my   precious   Lord   to   see   again   thy   radiant   face,   to   bask   forever

in   thy   light;   thy   shield   that   crushed   the   heal   of   night,   before   the   awesome   bounty

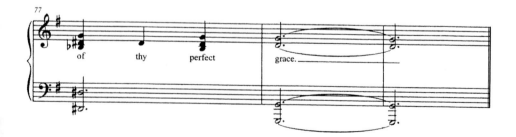

of   thy   perfect   grace.

May Heavenly Father favor us and bless us. May He safeguard us at all times and illuminate His countenance upon us. In these troubled times, pray always that He will establish peace in the hearts of mankind.

— *From Blessings Of The Torah*